PURITY
OF HEART

MOTIVES and VALUES

BERT M. FARIAS

CONTENTS

PREFACE..7

1. WHEN LIGHT BECOMES DARKNESS..............................11
2. HYPE OR HOLINESS..19
3. BREAKTHROUGHS OR BACKSLIDINGS.........................27
4. NO HOLINESS, NO HARVEST....................................35
5. WANTED: HOLY PRIESTS.......................................43
6. THE HURT THAT HEALS..55
7. THE MASTER ON MOTIVES.....................................69
8. WHEN THE NARROW BECOMES BROAD.......................75
9. MOTIVES AND VALUES...83
10. THE HEAL THAT HURTS.......................................93
11. TRUE OR FALSE...101
12. FALSE HUMILITY AND CARNAL SUSPICION.................113
13. OLD LEAVEN, NEW LUMP.....................................121
14. THE DAY OF DISTINCTION...................................131
15. HOLY FEAR, HOLY FIRE......................................137
16. HOLY BONDAGE, HOLY LIBERTY.............................145
17. KEEPING THE MOTIVES OF YOUR HEART PURE.......151

CONCLUSION: LOVE - THE MIGHTY MOTIVATOR..........157

REFERENCES...161
ABOUT THE AUTHOR...163

PREFACE

Scripture tells us that only the pure in heart shall see God (Mat 5:8). This book's title, *Purity of Heart,* bears this out in every chapter.

The phrase, "the end *justifies* the means" is often heard. Wicked and dishonest means are used frequently to reach a desired end. But in Christendom this phrase should be changed to say, "The end *purifies* the means." If our end is *truly* to glorify God, then our means or motives will always be pure. Thus you have the subtitle of this book, "*Motives and Values.*"

This book is surgical. It cuts you apart, and then puts you back together. If you yield yourself to the Surgeon's knife, *veils* will be removed from your heart and *scales* will fall from your eyes. The fruit of it all will be clear sight. You will see the Lord!

Years ago, while still in Bible school, I heard a quote from one of my most respected teachers, which became seed for the book you now hold. It went something like this: "A man can preach a great sermon, and actually get a demerit for it because his motive was wrong. An author can write a great book and get a demerit for it because his motive, too, was wrong (I'm searching my heart with fear and trembling as I write this now). A person can sing a great song and also get a demerit for it because of wrong motives. Oh, how important this principle is in our Christian walk!" That statement made a great impact on me early in my Christian life.

Then, more recently, I read a word preached by Smith Wigglesworth that also confirms the importance of this book's message. During a question and answer time with Bible school students, Wigglesworth was asked a question having to do with knowing the leading of the Spirit. Here is the question and Wigglesworth's answer, just as it was recorded:

Question: "When we have a strong impression to do a thing, how do we know that it is the Holy Spirit speaking?"

Answer: "Hundreds of people are in this dilemma, to get to the mind of God. The first thing you must always keep in mind is that when you are living in the perfect will of God, you only will that which is purposed in His will. If you are not living in that perfect attitude toward God, you may have any amount of thoughts of your own nature that you will find brings you into difficulty. It is the easiest thing to get the mind of the Lord when your whole heart's only desire is the will of the Lord. That will save you from a thousand troubles.

Are you so in touch with God that the desire of your mind is purity regarding that thing you want to be done? Has it the sanction of purity? Would Christ desire that thing? If so, the moment you pray, you will have the witness of the Spirit and it will coincide with the will of God.

But the difficulties are that people want the Lord's revelation in a carnal manner or a carnal life or where there is some human thing. Ask yourself these things: Why you are in the meeting, why you want to live, why you want to go to the conventions, why you want to be pastor, why you are anxious this morning. Act and you will be freed. If I can find out that I want to be in Angeles Temple for anything but for the glory of God and the extension of His kingdom, then I am in sin. If I want to be heard, I am wrong. If I want to be seen, I am wrong. If I want to be honored, I am wrong. But if I want Christ, if I want to preach because I want to advocate His glorious Gospel, if I want to be seen only because I want to exhibit His Spirit, if I am here for the advancement of the glory of Christ, then things are as easy as possible." (Liardon, 1998. p. 11-12)

What a word! My strongest admonishment to you for these last days is this: Keep the motives of your heart pure. And with all your heart, pursue holiness for without holiness no man shall see the Lord (Heb 12:14). A fresh vision of Jesus is worth it all!

ARE YOU READY FOR THE JUDGMENT SEAT OF CHRIST?

The great revelation in this book is this: The basis of all God's judgments lies in the motives of the heart.

*For we must all appear and be **revealed as we are** before the judgment seat of Christ, so that each one may receive [his pay] according to what he has done in the body, whether good or evil, [**considering what his purpose and motive have been, and what he has achieved, been busy with and given himself and his attention to accomplishing**]. (2 Cor 5:10 Amp)*

*So do not make any hasty or premature judgments before the time when the Lord comes [again], for He will both bring to light the secret things that are [now hidden] in darkness and disclose and expose the [secret] aims **(motives and purposes) of hearts**. Then every man will receive his [due] commendation from God. (1 Cor 4:5 Amp)*

*So don't make judgments about anyone ahead of time—before the Lord returns. For he will bring our darkest secrets to light and will reveal our **private motives**. Then God will give to each one whatever praise is due. (1 Cor 4:5 NLT)*

*It's no light thing to know that we'll all one day stand in that place of Judgment. **That's why we work urgently with everyone we meet to get them ready to face God.** (2 Cor 5:11 Msg)*

Now if anyone builds on this foundation with gold, silver, precious stones, wood, hay, straw, each one's work will become clear; for the Day will declare it, __*because it will be revealed by fire; and the fire will test each one's work, of what sort it is*__. *If anyone's work which he has built on it endures, he will receive a reward. If anyone's work is burned, he will suffer loss; but he himself will be saved, yet so as through fire.* (1 Cor 3:12-15 NKJ)

Chapter One
WHEN LIGHT BECOMES DARKNESS

Take heed that the light which is in you is not darkness. (Lk 11:35)

A certain "no name" minister arranged an appointment to meet with the "chief ruler" of a large "gospel" ministry. The man was hurting and needed a lift. Great discouragement brought on by a troubled marriage and a rebellious teenage son gripped him. Moreover, harsh words from a close associate aimed at ruining his already tarnished reputation wounded him deeply. This betraying blow knocked the wind out of him and made him contemplate giving up altogether on life and ministry.

Standing on the brink of a total collapse of his life, this minister waited patiently at the request of the "chief ruler's" personal secretary, to see him. In his broken heart there were flashes of light and hope that he would receive just what he needed from this ruler. The counsel of the Lord or a great word of wisdom and encouragement was what he anticipated from this person he greatly admired. He was so thankful just to be able to have an audience with this internationally known figure and very busy man.

Finally, the time for the much-awaited visit came. This "no name" minister walked into the "chief ruler's" lavish office. A sparkling marble walkway laid and lined through the midst of luscious lavender carpet was his path to the leather-covered armchair in which he was to sit. What a beautiful office! Exquisite paintings draped every wall, state-of-the-art equipment filled one corner of the room, unique and rare decorative ornaments flavored the atmosphere, and a very expensive oriental hand-woven rug surrounded the massive mahogany, gold-trimmed desk, from where this ruler welcomed his guests.

11

Greetings were quickly exchanged, and then the ruler casually began sharing the purpose of his own life and mission. He dwelt there awhile, and with somewhat of an air of self-admiration, he reflected back on the call of God he received as a young boy. Moments turned to minutes as the ruler continued to immerse himself into his own accomplishments and achievements. He spoke of the establishment and the growth of his worldwide ministry. He described how it supplied blessing and provision for the peoples of many nations.

Slowly this "no name" begins to feel a tinge of nausea. The initial sweetness in his mouth started to sour in his belly. The room, sparkling with high-priced décor, now looked dark and oppressive. A look of indulgence seemed to overcome the ruler's entire countenance as he continued talking, but to the "no name's" ears, his sayings no longer mattered. They had become muddled mutterings and vain babbling. Like a stone on water, his heart sank.

The ruler never once asked the "no name" of his own life and troubles. Not once did he inquire of his trials and struggles. Although minutes continued to pass, the "no name" had not yet been given an opportunity to pour out his heart and ask for counsel and prayer. Oh, he was sure that sooner or later the ruler would stop and inquire, but his apparent insensitive attitude had already raised too many doubts in his mind. Frankly, if first impressions meant anything, he was turned off. He saw through the deceptive outward veil and didn't like the view. The uncaring disposition of this "chief ruler" now wanted to make the "no name" run.

At last he was asked the purpose of his visit, but by now it didn't matter. The "no name" passed over spilling the truth of his heart, and instead chose the way of least vulnerability. He no longer felt comfortable in this ruler's presence. After engaging in some more useless verbiage, the "no name" gladly excused himself and went on his way.

Finally, in his parked automobile and well away from the glitter and veneer, with his whole upper body slouched over the steering wheel, this "no name" wept and wailed under the deepened agony of his broken heart. He had entered so desperate for help and encouragement, only to withdraw disappointed, feeling at best more helpless and discouraged. The light he expected to receive was darkness. Selfishness clouded the "chief ruler's" world and his "gospel" ministry.

But wait a minute. Is it just the big and the rich, the popular and the prominent whose life can become so insensitive and self-centered? It just so happened that this "no name" minister was from a large church full of people and even ministers he could have sought for help. But he was afraid in the "home" environment to expose himself. He feared the people of his own sheepfold would judge him. No one seemed to care anyway.

How many of us have been in the "no name's" shoes, when we longed for someone around us to give us some word of encouragement and to show some care? How many times have we longed for someone to take genuine interest and concern in what was going on in our lives, and yet all they could talk about was themselves? And how many of us have been on the other end of things, when we should have been the ones reaching out to some poor, hurting, and discouraged soul, we failed to do so due to our own self-focus?

All of us, if we're not careful, can be so immersed in our own lives, our own world, our own family, and our own dreams and desires that we lose the very heart of God. People all around us need us. We cannot help everyone, but we can help the ones God calls us to help. But how can we hear any call from God when we're so consumed with ourselves? How can we hear well away from the glitter and veneer, the voice of compassion, when we're so concerned about our own comfort and convenience?

Our once cultivated hearts can quickly become a wasteland without the fear of the Lord and right motives.

13

Has your heart become a wasteland---a swamp that takes in but never gives out? Is the stench of selfishness polluting your life? Have the former clear waters of your once loving heart become muddied with self-centeredness? Receiving without ever releasing will keep those waters receding until what was meant to be a clean-flowing river becomes a dirty well.

The true spirit of Christianity is summed up in John 3:16. God so loved He *gave*...to others. What God gave was a manifestation of His love. But wait another minute. Even though it seems very unlikely that a person could ever truly love without giving, it is very possible to give without loving. Actually, it happens quite frequently.

One time a missionary friend of mine received a letter from a sponsoring church requesting a written report of accountability in exchange for the monthly support he received. My friend understood that some churches required this, so he would prepare reports when he had some time. However, when he failed to find time in his busy schedule to immediately respond to the church's request, he received a second letter from them requesting the same. The second letter reproved the missionary for the reporting delay. They even threatened to stop his support unless they received the accounting they required. My friend then disclosed to me the amount of this church's support -- $25.00 per month. This church was guilty of giving without loving. With that attitude they should have kept their money, because God will not recognize that kind of giving.

God's unconditional love is the basis of all true giving. Love simply gives because it loves. But this goes much deeper. We can preach and teach the Word of God without loving. We can sing and prophesy without loving. We can even pray without loving. The scriptures tell us that we can give all of our money and goods to feed the poor, and even sacrifice our bodies to be burned, and do so without love (1 Cor 13:3). Yes, we can sacrifice and go without, and yet do all this with no love motivating us! How can this be? One can sacrifice and do good, all with a personal agenda attached to it. *Giving is only honorable when the motive is pure.*

Here is another example. A church recognizes its visitors on Sunday morning. With every visitor's kind permission, and as a token of appreciation for their visit, the church arranges for the delivery of a special gift to each visiting family's home. Knowing that we are commanded to love not in word only but in deed, this is a wonderful gesture of love. But hold on. We know words can deceive. Sometimes they mean nothing at all. But what about deeds? Could supposed good deeds be used to manipulate someone? Are we really concerned about people's welfare, or do we just want more people in our church? After all, more people means more money, and with more money the church can do much more.

Here's one more. A new church is started in the community. The pastor has a vision to build up the work. He longs to be a success in this pioneer effort, so he develops a plan for aggressive outreach. The people are mobilized for active, ongoing door-to-door evangelism. They diligently map out an area and are determined to knock on the door of every home. They introduce themselves as members of this new church, which they say is there to help the community. It's a tireless work for only the truly committed. But wait. Do they really care about these people, or are they just knocking on doors to build up the church? What is our truest motivation for evangelism? God's motive to give was so we wouldn't perish (John 3:16). We are no better than any of the cults if all we do is win converts to build up our work.

Listen to a voice from the past:

Nothing, which is selfish, is Christian. There is nothing faithful in any selfish act. A man may just as much commit sin in praying, reading the Bible, or going to a service as in anything else, if his motive is selfish. Suppose

15

a man prays with a view to simply promote his own happiness. Is that God fearing? It is no more than attempting to make God his Almighty Servant! It is nothing but an attempt to put the universe and God in a position to make the self happy. It is the greatest degree of wickedness. It is so far from piety and goodness that it is superlative wickedness. (Finney, 1984. p. 119-120)

Our hearts can become hard and calloused over a period of time if we don't keep our motives pure. Selfishness then breeds and builds in our lives. The cycle can be quickly reversed if we will begin preferring others before ourselves.

Years ago, while traveling in the States and raising funds for our mission in Africa, my wife and I stayed in the home of some friends for a number of weeks. You can really find out a lot about yourself when you are either a guest in someone's home or a host in your own. Know this, a guest who wears out his welcome and a host who lacks hospitality are a very poor combination, and can quickly create tension in any home. During this particular stay I got in a rut. Instead of having a servant's posture, I developed a sitting chief's posture.

One day my complaints about our hosts' lack of hospitality and service began to grieve me. In my self-centeredness I had failed, up to this time, to see what the real problem was. It was not our hosts' lack of hospitality, but my lack of gratitude and appreciation. I resolved then and there to be a servant to our hosts. One afternoon while they were out, I mowed their lawn and did some yard work. What a difference this one act of love and service made, both in my heart, and especially in theirs! Immediate change followed as the tension in their home turned to joy and liberty, all because I got my eyes off myself and on others. Instead of getting, I began giving. This is the real Christian spirit. It can start with your spouse, your children, your neighbors and those around you.

Listen to another voice from the past:

The greatest manifestation of the Holy Ghost baptized life ever given to the world was not in the preaching of the apostles; it was not in the wonderful manifestations of God that took place at their hands. *It was in the unselfishness manifested by the church* (author's italics). Think of it! Three thousand Holy Ghost baptized Christians in Jerusalem from the day of Pentecost onward who loved their neighbors' children as much as their own, who were so anxious for fear their brethren did not have enough to eat, that they sold their estates, brought the money, laid it at the apostles' feet and said, 'Distribute it. Carry the glow and the fire and the wonder of this divine salvation to the whole world.' That showed what God had wrought in their hearts. Oh, I wish we could arrive at that place, where this church were baptized to that degree of unselfishness. (Quote by John G. Lake) (Lindsay, p. 21)

A *pure heart* is a *heart pure in motive*. More than anything, holiness is a state of heart. A perfect heart is a heart striving to be perfect in motive. Every Christian has light and revelation from God in varying degrees, and each one is only required to walk in the light he has. What is required of you is what has been given to you. Light becomes darkness when the motive becomes impure.

Here is a final example of this. I read an interesting account one time about a group of Christian tourists in a foreign country. Jumping out of a bus to photograph a famous Christian personality, all the while ignoring the obvious condition and need of an old lady as she walked tiredly along the side of the road, carrying a heavy load of firewood on her head. Here is the strong rebuke that was given to them by the man of God these tourists wished to photograph.

You met that poor old lady with a heavy load on her

head. You didn't give her a prayer, you didn't give her a Bible, you didn't give her a gospel tract, you didn't give her a penny of money---no one offered to lift her load. All you did was stand around and photograph her. *I don't know what brand of Christianity you are, but whatever it is I'm on the opposite side. Whatever brand you are, I'm not* (author's italics). We haven't been called to go around the world photographing the world, but we've been called by Jesus to go into the world and preach the gospel to every person...to care for the naked, the hungry, to visit the sick, those in prison, to be friends. This is an abomination...photographing the world and doing nothing for God. Touring the world with Bibles in your pockets, having devotions in the hotel while the world around you is hungry and lost and on the road to hell! (Blessitt, 1985. p. 336)

The light in these people had become darkness (Mat 6:23). We may be casual toward an incident like this, thinking that perhaps we are not of this company. But I challenge you to look closely at your life. Consider the judgments of God. Note very carefully the distinction made at Judgment Day between the sheep and the goats (Mat 25:31-46). Remember that Christianity is easy to fake. Are you involved in meeting the needs of others? Are you praying, giving, and caring for others? Where is your focus, on you or on them? From the moment you awake in the morning until you lay back down to sleep at night, are you looking to be blessed or are you focused on being a blessing?

Which brand of Christianity are you living?

Don't be a goat who fakes the faith now, only to forfeit the future later.

Take heed that the light, which is in you, be not darkness. (Lk 11:35)

Chapter Two
HYPE OR HOLINESS

Are these popular ministerial personalities great in the sight of the Lord or only in the sight of man? Are they really known in heaven or only on the earth? Are they God anointed or self appointed? Is it ministry they deliver or another subtle form of hype?

Many who are great in the sight of the Lord are living in cottages and hovels, and are scarcely known, unless to a few neighbors equally obscure. (Quote by William Jay) (Brown, 1993. p. 168)

Believers, especially Christian ministers, need a baptism of clear seeing and holy discerning. Our ministry marketing budget may be soaring high, but our perception can sometimes be so low. Our motives need refinement. The refiner's fire is near the door. Will you open it? Can you see the narrow way to holiness? Or is all the smoke blocking your view?

Before me now I see the impression I saw months ago. There are two scenes. One is of a clear and sunny horizon lined with an endless row of people. The other is of a vast forest. Dense fog covers the forest, and out of the fog comes the Lord Jesus Christ. Christ, for the most part, is not found among the general populace. People have to really look to recognize Him.

Think about it. Our Savior was not born in a big metropolis, but in the small town of Bethlehem. And He grew up in the despised country of Galilee. He was not born in a palace where kings are, but in a lowly stable. The wise men had to really search and diligently follow the star to find Him. When Jesus entered into ministry, it is written that He had no place to lay His head (Lk 9:58). He did not have a ministry headquarters. He died a criminal's death on a cross, naked and nearly alone. His grave was a borrowed tomb. His throne was an invisible one hidden from the multitudes of those who were healed and delivered through His ministry. He was called meek and lowly; certainly not the description fitting for a king. But today, ministry is so different.

A church brings in a special speaker. He's known all over so the people flock to hear him. They come from everywhere, every night. At the meetings they jump, sing, and shout. They hear the newest revelation proclaimed with jubilation. The people are saying of the special speaker:

> He's on T.V.
> I love his personality
> His ministry is so big,
> His clothes I really dig
> He's so wonderful!
> And his wife looks so smart
> Her latest hit song
> Is at the top of the chart
> Oh, I love to hear him speak,
> And I hate to see him go
> Maybe he'll stay another week,
> Or speak again on his daily show.

The same church brings in a name unknown. The people stay away by the droves. A few faithful gather to hear the Word of God. They long for holiness and a vision of Jesus. With a broken heart, the little "no name" preacher weeps for lost souls as he delivers a word from God.

The big personality was sent by man. The little "no name" was sent by God. The crowds who came from miles away came to hear a man. The smaller group came seeking Jesus. One set of meetings produced much excitement but no fruit of holiness. The other smaller meetings generated far less excitement but resulted in a brokenness and a lasting work of holiness in those who came. This may seem like an extreme example, but it makes the point.

Just because someone or something is big doesn't mean it's godly (and it is also understood that bigness is not tantamount to ungodliness either). In fact, it's a greater test of our devotion to be big (whatever "big" means to us) and yet remain holy, than it is to be small (whatever "small" means to us) and holy. And let's not forget that smallness is not equivalent to godliness either. Discerning the difference between hype and holiness is what's important. But we are so often fooled by the "big" while being unaware and undiscerning of the "small."

Holiness is not only sought but bought: "Buy of Me gold tried in the fire that you may be rich" (Rev 3:17). Have you been tried in the fire? Have you tested your teachings? Have you experienced and even suffered for the truth you believe? Truth is to be bought, not sold. We sell the truth when we sell our souls to pleasure, profit, and earthly popularity. We buy the truth when we are tried and found true, when we suffer with godly sorrow the pains of our personal Gethsemanes, and yet remain private about them. When we allow God to strip us of all glory seeking and subtle pride, we are buying the truth.

Too many today are selling messages they never bought. When we minister forth from what we've personally experienced or suffered, the Spirit will produce a far greater effect of holiness in the hearers. The deeper the suffering is, or has been; usually the more perfect the obedience. The more fiery the trials, and the deeper the burning, the purer and the richer the vessel becomes.

This is what we must understand: God's measuring gauge and standard of holiness is so different than man's. Bigness and smallness are terms not found in Christ. Here is the criterion for holiness: Is Christ made visible? Is He seen and heard? Is the ministration of Christ being imparted? Are the people changed more into His likeness? Are they manifesting a spirit of holiness and being filled with the fruits of righteousness? Are they paying less credence to men and personalities and reverencing God?

Years ago I was ministering a series of meetings for a church in an outdoor tent. Every night I preached, called people to repentance, and prayed for the sick. One day in the middle of these meetings the host pastor asked me if I moved in the gifts of the Spirit. I answered him that on occasion we saw certain manifestations of the Holy Spirit. I knew when he asked this question that he was disappointed with the meetings even though people were repenting and the sick that were there were getting healed. The gifts of the Spirit were not in clear manifestation, but people were still receiving salvation and healing by faith in the Word of God. Part of this pastor's problem was that while he looked for the spectacular he was missing the supernatural that was there all along. Anyway, out of his dissatisfaction this pastor would prophesy to a few people every night after I'd finish with my preaching and altar ministry.

And why, I wondered, did he have to do this almost every service? Was it really because he wanted to see people blessed? Or was there another subtle reason or motive lurking in this pastor's heart?

In one of the meetings he called a young couple forward and began to prophesy to them of their call and future ministry, and how God wanted to use them mightily. What this pastor wasn't fully aware of was the number of problems this young couple had in their home and marriage. They were nowhere near ready for ministry or even to hear a word like he gave concerning their call to ministry, whether it was accurate or not. I had sensed that this prophecy was not fully accurate, and certainly not in season. Months later I found out that this couple left their church prematurely to try and enter the full-time ministry. Their home life and marriage were still a mess, and their greatest need was to mature more in a local setting so they could develop some character. Since receiving this prophecy, I heard their lives became even more complicated and an even greater mess.

Due to hype, two lives were set back and maybe even ruined because of a minister's desire to make something happen outside of the will and timing of God. *Hype fakes the happening while delaying true holiness.* Hype is infinitely more dangerous than we can ever imagine because it lies to us and tells us that something great is happening, when in fact, there is very little going on. This example is just one isolated account of what really happens on a much wider scale.

As missionaries, my wife and I have been a part of evangelistic campaigns over the years (both our own and those of others) that would produce much excitement but little holiness. There were genuine miracles, too, and the evangelists were good men of God, but the conversions and lasting fruit these campaigns would bring were very minimal - so much so that it would make us wonder. Often evangelists would boast of the number of decisions made for Christ in a particular city. Their statistics were gathered from the number of hands that went up when they would ask how many of them wanted to go to heaven. Then the evangelist would lead them in a sinner's prayer. But we lived there and found that the churches were not really much fuller in attendance than before the campaign. I struggled with this for years, trying to find an answer. I reasoned, "Well, Jesus had a miracle ministry and still, at the end of it all, there were only a few that were really true disciples. He said only one of four persons would bear any fruit after hearing and even receiving the gospel (Mat 13:18-23)." But I wanted to know why it had to be this way when history tells us that a man like Charles Finney had nearly 80% of his converts stay true to God.

Part of the answer I found had to do with the holiness which God desired to birth in the will and heart of man through both a new kind of prayer (deep intercession) and a new kind of preaching. After much questioning I began to find some answers. I found that the key to a true and lasting conversion lay again in the *motive of the heart.*

A false convert is one who claims belief in Jesus but whose heart and life remains unchanged.

These likewise are the ones sown on stony ground who, when they hear the word, immediately receive it with gladness; and they have no root in themselves, and so endure only for a time. Afterward, when tribulation or persecution arises for the word's sake, immediately they stumble. Now these are the ones sown among thorns; they are the ones who hear the word, and the cares of this world, the deceitfulness of riches, and the desires for other things entering in choke the word, and it becomes unfruitful. (Mk 4:16-19)

In the Old Testament Pharaoh submitted to God's demands through Moses to let Israel go only when the plagues became unbearable, but as soon as things lightened up Pharaoh reneged on his promise. His supposed submission was insincere. The motive of his heart was only to escape further trouble and hardship. It was a temporary deal. It was what is commonly called "fire escape religion." This happens quite frequently with lost souls, who receive the word gladly to escape their trouble and get relief from their hardship, but are insincere.

Then there are those in a second category of wrong heart motives who come to Christ solely for the blessings and benefits of Christianity. They want a better and improved lifestyle with no regard to the demands and purposes of Christ. Everyone wants peace and joy. Everyone wants to go to heaven. But very few want to truly serve the Lord. This wrong heart motivation is equivalent to using and manipulating a person in order to get some benefit from them. It's a relationship based on resources, or supposed friendship based on funds. It's an insult to the blood of Jesus and to His Lordship. In His earthly ministry Jesus never enticed sinners to a commitment based on benefits. The blessing of eternal life is enough!

Finally, there is a third category of false conversions. This group actually believes in Christ, but lack a genuine heart loyalty to Him because of the persecution and rejection they know they will have to suffer for the sake of the gospel. For example, we found this attitude prevalent in Muslim nations where young men and women believed in Jesus, but would not commit wholeheartedly to Him for fear of being ostracized from their families. And this attitude is not just found among Muslims, but among many others who simply will not esteem Christ above the persecution they may have to experience for their faith.

Herein lies the key to a genuine conversion: the esteem of Christ above everything else. Paul esteemed Christ and His glory so much that suffering hardship and persecution could not compare to it (Rom 8:18). Moses esteemed the reproach of Christ greater than the treasures and pleasures of Egypt (Heb 11:25-26). *The seed of the gospel remains under protective cover, taking root, growing, and bearing fruit in those who continue esteeming the person of Jesus Christ greater than anything else.* Pure heart motives are revealed by a person's total surrender to Christ.

Esteem. Think of what it means. When my family and I travel long and late hours together by automobile, I will not fall asleep at the wheel. Esteem for not only my life, but for my family's life, either keeps me awake or will make me pull over and sleep. Christ *esteemed* mankind so much that he endured even the death of the cross. Our death to the flesh and the world, and our surrender to the Lord, is evidence of our high esteem for Him. This is the motive that wins God's heart, seals and secures a person's salvation, and will continue to sanctify him.

Years ago in a meeting, I saw the outward manifestation of what really happens when a heart truly turns toward God. A man answered my invitation to come and be saved. After I had prayed with him and led him to Jesus, I offered him a free tape series to begin to feed his faith. Upon receiving the tapes, the man gave thanks and then did something that brought me great joy. With a holy glow on his face, he told me that he was going to share the tapes with others in the church. Here was a man, not even minutes old in the Lord, and his heart was already turned toward others--evidence of God's love that

25

had just been poured into his heart by the Holy Ghost (Rom 5:5). The motive of his heart was to give more than to get. This is true holiness and purity of heart.

Chapter Three
BREAKTHROUGHS OR BACKSLIDINGS

Someone once said that a believer can lose in ten minutes what he gained in one year. Only a spiritual man could understand such a statement. How is it possible? Before we delve into the spiritual, let me put this to you on a natural level. A brief few moments of pleasure in an adulterous affair can cost a man or a woman everything - their marriage, their children, their good reputation, and even their lives and peace. To be carnally minded is death, but to be spiritually minded is life and peace (Rom 8:6).

Just as a man could forfeit his position as a husband and a father, so can a believer through sin, disobedience, and negligence forfeit places and positions gained in the Spirit. Christian, be warned! Carelessness costs. Watchfulness pays.

While we were missionaries in Africa we hired security personnel to guard and keep our house and compound from thieves and intruders. As in the Bible, we called them watchmen. In a short few moments of sleep a watchman could allow a valuable fortune of goods and property to be stolen and lost. In Old Testament times, gates to a city could be plummeted by the enemy and in a brief span of time that city, besieged and conquered. Are you guarding your gates?

In our home in Africa, we always locked our gate(s) at night, but at times intruders would find a place to climb over the wall. I've heard of slick thieves sneaking past two hired and armed guards to raid and plunder the luxurious home of some government dignitary. While the armed guards slept, the thieves got in over the wall. Are you watching your walls?

The servant who is not looking and expecting his master's soon return is evil and worthy of many stripes (Lk 12:46-47). The one found waiting (v 36), watching (v 37), and ready (v 40) is called faithful and wise (v 42-43), and appointed as a ruler. Positions are gained in the Spirit according to our faithfulness, obedience, and wisdom. Positions are lost according to our disobedience and our lack of preparedness and readiness. Are you gaining or losing?

Ananias was ready, so the Lord served him a vision and sent him on a great assignment (Acts 9). Those who are looking for Jesus are now being *served* and *sent*. Assignments are being granted according to our alertness. The faithful are watching. The wise are waiting. Visions and dreams are being released. Visitations are being received. The Spirit is poured out. Demons are cast out. Angels await orders. Missionary agents cross borders. Arise, saint, from your sleeping quarters! The Master is at the door.

Guard the gate! Watch the wall! Don't be late when you hear the call!

Many believers are asking God for a breakthrough, but God is handing out assignments that lead to breakthroughs. Why do you want a breakthrough when you haven't even fulfilled your assignment?

Spiritual authority is increased, entrance is granted into treasured rooms (I'm speaking spiritually), and special privileges, rewards, and blessings are given as a result of your obedience to the Lord. Every day you must go forward. Every day you must gain ground in God. You must deny yourself in order to make spiritual progress. You must refuse all that is not pure and holy.

Think about this. What if Abraham had not been willing to offer up Isaac? What if Joseph had not forgiven Potiphar's wife and remained bitter? What if David had not refused to retaliate against Saul? What if Jesus had not overcome the temptations in the wilderness? Let me tell you what would've never been. Abraham would have never been the father of nations. Joseph would have never been prime minister of

Egypt. David would have never been king. And Jesus, too, would have never been Lord and Savior.

A believer can gain or forfeit certain things by his actions or his attitude. And remember, to whom much is given, much is also required. Under certain circumstances one big act of disobedience can cost you. Moses struck the rock twice instead of speaking to it as God had commanded (Num 20:11-13), and he was denied entrance into the Promised Land. Achan transgressed the covenant and took of the spoils of the enemy which God forbid. He, his family, and their possessions were burned in the fire (Jos 7:15, 24-25). Uzzah touched the ark, which was also forbidden, and lost his life (2 Sam 6:6-7). Ananias and Sapphira lied to the Holy Spirit and also lost their lives (Acts 5). This is not a game we're playing. It is a war in which we're engaging. Casualties are real. If you die in the field of battle, may you die honorably. Let it not be because of your own carelessness or negligence to fulfill a high command from the Captain of your salvation. When the glory of God returns to the church, we are going to have to be much more sober and careful about sin and disobedience. Why not start being that way now?

To him who overcomes I will give him some of the hidden manna to eat. And I will give him a white stone, and on the stone a new name written which no one knows except him who receives it. (Rev 2:17)

The one who overcomes is rewarded. In this raging war there will always be obstacles to overcome. Here is how it works. God takes you to school and you must make the grades to advance to another level. Your sanctification and not your salvation is the issue. You must constantly overcome the three areas that Jesus overcame: the pride of life, the lust of the eyes, and the lust of the flesh. God will not allow you to be tested or tempted beyond what you are able (1 Cor 10:13), and He will always make a way of escape. He is not a hard taskmaster either. His mercies are new every morning. If you don't make the grades, however, you'll just keep taking the same test over and over again. If you're faithful in a little, God will entrust you with more. If you're faithful in what is another man's, God will give you what is your own (Lk 16:10, 12). Best of all, God has sent the Holy Spirit to help you be an overcomer.

In my life over the years, I have noticed, after overcoming a real test or obstacle, that there was always a blessing and a sort of inheritance that would follow sometime later. For instance, on a very practical level, I did many jobs as a single man before entering the ministry that I absolutely hated. Yet God wouldn't let me quit until I learned to be content in that job. And if I got fired or dismissed dishonorably, I would not receive any particular special blessing from the Lord. In other words, nothing would be gained. But whenever I finished out my season and maintained the proper grade and attitude, God would always reward me.

One of the first jobs I had as a Christian was working as a retail jewelry sales clerk in a mall. My boss was a very demanding woman who, at times, could be very unreasonable. One time she made me pay for a $2.00 error that I made on a sale. I thought she was going to kill me when I told her that I didn't have any money. Time after time I felt like I was treated unjustly by this woman. And time after time I had to forgive her. The Lord would not let me hold any kind of grudge against her. One day He even impressed upon me to give her a hug. Have you ever tried to hug someone that you wanted to punch? As a new convert known for being unusually high tempered, I found this to be a real test. By God's grace I passed, and shortly after moved on to another job assignment in my life, and, wouldn't you know it, another test.

Let me tell you about this one, too. It was advertised as a temporary employment opportunity of only a few weeks, so I knew that whatever I did there, good or bad, I'd be gone in a few weeks. I also knew, however, because the Lord was teaching me, that if I failed this assignment, I'd be delayed in receiving the next favor or privilege the Lord had planned for me. Just when I'd think I was out of the woods, so to speak, God would put me through another gauntlet.

This temporary opportunity was in telephone sales. Again, I did not like it; I hired on out of necessity. At first, it was so hard to smile, especially when the great telephone sales presentation they taught me was rejected over and over again by irate and unkind people. Again, the Lord dealt with me about my attitude. Soon, out of approximately fifteen sales agents, I became the most positive person on the staff. Little did I know that these things would later prepare me for life on the mission field. Oh, how important are those little steps of obedience! They play a great part in training you and shaping your character and future.

Lack of obedience in one area will affect other areas of your life. The law of sowing and reaping applies everywhere, in everything, in every day of your life. God is a covenant God. Yes, He is merciful and forgiving, but only when you are, too (Mat 6:14-15). It's not that God ever stops loving you, or that His love is conditional, or that He will never bless you based purely on His mercy, but His covenant is conditional. Promotion in His kingdom is based on our stewardship and performance. His blessings and rewards are conditional. I'm told that there are thousands of promises in the Bible, each with a condition. When you only preach the promises, you become guilty of taking away from the Word. When you modify or alter the conditions, you become guilty of adding to the Word. How you treat His covenant and keep His commandments affects how high you go in your calling. Jesus would never have moved into power until He had passed the wilderness temptations. Jesus would never have moved on to His high priestly ministry if He had not overcome Gethsemane.

You must prove to God, not only by your willingness to keep your part of the covenant, but by your obedience. Faith without works is always dead (Jam 1:21-22). How can a Christian pray for revival and lost souls if he's not reaching out to the lost himself? How can God use you to do big things when you won't obey him in the little things?

Not too long ago I went with a pastor friend of mine to visit another pastor from a nearby city. Among other things, we went to ask for the use of this other pastor's church building for a service one night a week. Since this other pastor didn't know my friend, I went and introduced them and vouched for his character. Well, I knew that this other pastor was praying and believing God for a new building himself, so I had a sense that this was an open door for him to sow the use of his own building into another man's ministry. As a matter of fact, I knew that this pastor for whom I vouched was this other pastor's ticket into a new building. All he had to do was to sow the use of his own building one night per week into my friend. But guess what? He wouldn't do it. To this day he's still looking for his new building.

I could tell you story after story, just from my own short life and time in ministry, of how my obedience in one area birthed forth a blessing or a reward in another area. Favor, provision, and open doors resulted. Overcoming obstacles in order to obey God will release hidden manna, a white stone, and a new name written on the stone for the overcoming one (Rev 2:17). *Hidden manna* means secret things revealed. Greater wisdom, understanding, and revelation will be given. The divine influences of heaven will be upon your soul, and the wonder of Christ that you feel will not be understood except by those who are also overcoming. A *white stone* means freedom from guilt and condemnation. Overcoming the desires of the flesh by walking after the Spirit continually purifies your soul (1 Pet 1:22). The overcoming one will experience what others only know in theory. The *new name* is new character that is formed in you. It's evidence of your love and maturity. It's proof that you belong to God. It speaks of the intimacy you and God share.

Every time you overcome, more glory is manifested. Angels ministered to Jesus after He overcame the temptations in the wilderness (Mat 4:11). The more you overcome sin and the pride of life, the lust of the eyes, and the lust of the flesh, the less dominion and influence the world has upon you. Conversely, the more you yield to these things, the more influence the world will have over you. You see, all the time you are either gaining or losing position, place, and privilege in the Spirit. You're either going forward or sliding backward.

Of all that Jesus has given you, see that you lose nothing. Of all that Jesus has planned for you, see that you exercise due diligence to fulfill it. And if you've fallen and faltered like we all have at one time or another, believe for God to restore the fullness of His calling and will for your life. If you repent, He will show mercy and make your end sweet. Don't let your sins and shortcomings of yesterday hinder God's plan for today and tomorrow. Put your backslidings behind you, go forward now, and your breakthrough will come. While God does make big demands, He grants you His grace and ability to meet them, and in return, ministers big rewards (Mk 10:29-30).

Chapter Four
NO HOLINESS, NO HARVEST

For they have healed the hurt of the daughter of My people slightly (superficially), saying, 'Peace, peace!' when there is no peace. (Jer 8:11)

In much of today's contemporary Christian church, superficiality and hype have been a substitute for holiness, blinding many eyes to the true heart of God. Appearance, like any magical act, can be very deceptive. A spiritually "dead" people are easy to detect, but those with a reputation for being alive (but who are really just as dead) are not so obvious. The church at Sardis and the church at Laodicea were two such examples (Rev 3:1, 14). Hype's magic wand had hypnotized them from seeking true holiness. While superficial "churches" have a reputation for being alive, they all the time produce death.

Israel's spiritual physicians only touched the real need of the people superficially. There was very little weight and substance to what they ministered. Like the once popular restaurant commercial whose burgers are larger compared to others, the competition's customer cries, "Where's the beef?" How long can the contemporary church live on ice cream and cookies? Like spoiled children with seared consciences, many in the church have lost the power to even blush (Jer 8:12).

Spiritual children are given to folly. Only the rod of holiness will drive it from them. Their emotions are *thrilled* by hype, but their hearts can only be *tilled* by holiness. Some claim to be new creations but refuse to walk the righteous paths of old foundations. To them, the gospel is good news, but taking up the cross is bad news. Receiving blessings, yes! Denying self, no.

Superficial ministry is like a tree with leaves but no fruit. It produces hype without holiness. Superficial physicians without discernment will continue to *fill* prescriptions, but the patients remain *empty*. They are not recovering but regressing. They are not any healthier but sicker. They've been infected with a false sense of peace and security. Frankly, they've been *hurt by hype*.

Children of hype, who by this time ought to be teachers themselves, are the same way. They speak but do not hear. Their ears are uncircumcised, and they have no hunger for the true word of the Lord. While feasting on *peaceful* preaching (this is so dangerous in a time of war), they are swallowed up by *harmful* hype. They *coolly* play but never *truly* pray. They're out of sync with the times and seasons of God. If not warned, they will surely miss the time of visitation.

...And they sewed fig leaves together and made themselves coverings. (Gen 3:5)

Adam and Eve substituted fig leaves for the real glory that initially covered their nakedness. Superficial health experts specialize in sewing on more fig leaves while overlooking the real problem of nakedness, sin, and falsehood. They restock their shelves with their old prescriptions and fix up their old formulas instead of consulting with the Master Physician to hear what He is prescribing *now*. They repeat the age-old error in every new move of God. They wallow in the "old" while resisting the "new." True physicians detect the nakedness and recognize that only the true glory can cover.

Superficial high tech activity has fooled much of the church. Noise has cluttered their world. Busy, busy lifestyles have squashed their sensitivity. Bound by their schedules and long lists of to do's, their spiritual lives are like old cans of stale food whose time has expired. It's time to purchase some new cans with some fresh food. It's time to pour out the old wine and renew that old wineskin. It's time to seek the Lord.

Stop hiding in the "hype" and seek holiness. Hype causes us to unknowingly hide ourselves from the real presence of the Lord. Hype will even speak of holiness, but cannot produce it. It play-acts and imitates. Again, like little children, hype hides in the trees of false profession and pretentious activity while all the while resisting the voice of the Lord. Until it uncovers itself and comes out from behind the leaves of the trees we call churches, it will continue to just *play*. Attending church without attending to the presence of the Lord will kill any spiritual life. Proud church goers who don't have a fellowship with Jesus tend to hypocrisy, and they are unknowingly hiding from the presence of the Lord.

...When He (Jesus) came to it (the fig tree), He found nothing but leaves, for it was not the season for figs. (Mk 11:13)

Question. If it was not the season for figs then why would Jesus look for them? A commentary of mine tells me that on the fig tree the fruit is first formed, and then the leaves appear.

Jesus pronounced a curse on the fig tree, signifying judgment on Israel's false profession. Like Israel of old and many in the church today, they were not valiant for the truth (Jer 9:3). Hearken, church! Judgment is coming, and now is, on the church's false profession. The only hope for the fruit of holiness which the Owner looks for, are the keepers of the vineyard who delay judgment by fervent prayer, digging around and fertilizing the trees (Lk 13:6-9). False professors of faith are hypocrites, who like fruitless trees, waste the nutrients of the soil and take up space. Their hearts are hardened and desperately need cultivation in order to have a chance to repent and bear fruit.

It was not the beginning of the season for figs (Mk 11:13), but the end. Listen to Jeremiah lamenting:

The harvest is past, the summer is ended, and we are not saved. (Jer 8:20)

Astonishment gripped the prophet (v 21), a broken heart caused tears to gush from his eyes (Jer 9:1), because of the failing spiritual health of God's people and the shortage of viable and caring physicians. *There was no harvest because there was no holiness.* From the prophet to the priest, every one dealt falsely, and from the least to the greatest, everyone was given to covetousness (v 10).

An older gentleman went out to eat with a pastor friend of mine. During the meal, this gentleman suddenly got choked up and his countenance changed. Thinking, perhaps, the man was choking on his food, the pastor asked what was wrong. With tears in his eyes, the old man replied: "Oh, I'm just so thankful for the Blood of Jesus!" Then with that same sense of gratitude and brokenness, this tender man stood up in the crowded restaurant and began to testify of the wonder of Christ in his heart. Everyone listened as God's presence overflowed in that restaurant. He was enjoying the Savior in his heart, and others were receiving the overflow. Many were soundly impacted. A vision of God's holiness and of the true beauty of Christ will make you weep. *Holiness in a man's heart will always affect the harvest.*

Note the divine order to the work of evangelism and the conversion of sinners:

> *Create in me a clean heart, O God, and renew a steadfast spirit within me. Do not cast me away from Your presence, and do not take Your Holy Spirit from me. Restore to me the joy of Your salvation, and uphold me by Your generous Spirit. Then I will teach transgressors Your ways, and sinners shall be converted to You.* (Ps 51:10-13)

First, a clean heart and a steadfast spirit must be secured. Then the presence of the Holy Spirit will come, immediately followed by the restoration of the joy of salvation. And the final result will be the conversion of sinners. Simply put, revival and holiness in the lives of believers will lead to a harvest of souls won to Christ.

Evan Roberts was the young man who was instrumentally used by God to preach a message that began the great revival in Wales in the early 1900's. His message agrees with this divine sequence found in Psalm 51. Here are the four points to Evan's message, which helped to birth the forthcoming Welsh revival:

1. Confess every known sin to God and make right every sin known to man.
2. Remove doubtful habits from your life.
3. Obey the prompting of the Holy Spirit.
4. Go public with your witness of Christ.

I believe every revival begins with this type of message. It's as faithful as the day is long. It is repentance, followed by obedience, and then our obedience culminated by the public proclamation of the gospel. These four steps must take place in the depth of the hearts of God's people for them to birth forth change.

You see, there's a spiritual dimension of ministry that goes beyond any formula, theory, or methodology. General William Booth, founder of the Salvation Army, once gave some wise spiritual advice to a frustrated, ineffective group of evangelists by saying: "Try tears! Try tears!" (Hill, 1996. p. xvi)

One time, while helping a church with outreach on the streets of Rochester, New York, I saw a visible effect of what tears can do. Two sisters and I were standing on a street corner sharing the gospel with a man who was bound by the drug life. While we were talking to him, he seemed completely distracted. He kept looking around with restless anxiety. Our words were, for the most part, falling on deaf ears. Then, suddenly, one of the sisters began to plead with him. Tears rolled down her face as she shared her own conversion experience. This man's face and disposition totally changed. He was arrested by her compassion. I, too, was moved. I discovered a great secret that day. *Broken hearts open sealed hearts.* Unless believers are broken by the Holy Spirit and burdened for souls, much of our evangelistic activity will be fruitless.

Private tears and public tears will open men's hearts. Before the world can cry tears of repentance the church must learn to cry tears of intercession. The world's inability to cry ought to make us cry because, without tears of repentance, they will face eternal flames of punishment. A painless present will lead to a painful future.

Through the power of the Holy Spirit we must feel the pain of lost and hurting humanity. Their "numbness" to pain (their own or that of others) and to eternal issues of the soul has produced in them a strong resistance to any gospel message that lacks firepower. However, no amount of hardness is Holy Ghost fireproof. No measure of "numbness" is Holy Ghost impenetrable. We need hot tears of desperation for a cold and desperate generation. But the temple is void of tears and the hour is so late.

And Jesus went into Jerusalem and into the temple. So when He had looked around at all things, as the hour was already late, He went out to Bethany with the twelve. (Mk 11:11)

The fig tree Jesus cursed represented Israel, a nation of people with leaves but no fruit. At this late hour of Jesus' ministry when there should have been fruit in Israel and in the temple, there wasn't much. Likewise, at this now late hour when the church should be manifesting much more fruit, it isn't. What did those holy eyes of Jesus see in that temple? He saw a people like we see today who were professing faith and righteousness and maintaining external forms of godliness, but who through fraudulent practices made sacred things vile. He saw hypocrisy. He saw hype and superficiality. He saw lack of prayer. He saw lack of honor and reverence. He saw lack of holiness and power. Jesus saw a den of thieves (v 17).

Jesus was seeing, but He was also foreseeing. He knew that a confrontation in that same temple would mark the following day's events (Mk 11:15-17). That holy zeal would burn hot in the great heart of our Savior that night, and wait for its release the next day.

Jesus went to the fig tree, which once again represents Israel, because He was hungry. Jesus is now very hungry for a fruitful and faithful bride. He is inspecting her fruit. The fig tree episode would be a preview of things to come. Now watch this. Jesus looks behind the fig leaves. No fruit. Hmm. Just like the day before when He looked into the temple. No holiness in the temple. Hmm. The fig tree didn't have a chance when its Maker cursed it, but the temple would be purged and cleansed. Transition time was near.

A spiritual dream was given to a modern day handmaiden. A church was shown in transition. A stick bridge overgrown with tall jungle weeds which sprang through its cracks was the point of crossing. On the church side of the bridge was a near barren land. On the other side was a storehouse with a fresh kind of manna producing holiness unto the Lord, and a far greater power than they had ever known.

The transition was shaky for those who dared cross, but for those who refused, there would be much loss. The weeds prevented many from crossing. Some people even went part of the way but then turned back.

The meaning of the dream is prophetic. The church is at a crossroads. Every minister and member is now being required of the Lord to walk the stick bridge. Some have already gone to the other side. No man-made vehicle can cross. The journey must be made on foot, one step at a time. The bridge is narrow, and the way seems difficult, but in the end is life and holiness.

In this late hour, Jesus is now looking around at all things. He sees His Body, His temple, the Church. He sees the harvest and the world. Jesus is looking across that stick bridge of transition. It symbolizes the purging and purification of His temple. His consuming desire is for everyone to make the transition, but He knows not all will.

The spiritual seasons are changing. The summer is passing, and the winds of holiness are blowing. Even the fig leaves shall fade, and in the heat of His holiness there will be no shade. After the wind comes the fire. All that's holy will be refined, but the superficial will be devoured. In that day there will be no more sewing of fig leaves, no more hiding from the Omnipresent Seeker. He's coming, and He's counting (time is short). Everyone will be sought and caught (just like Adam and Eve in the garden after the fall). They will either be clothed in white or found naked. Will you be wanting?

Ready or not, here He comes...

Chapter Five
WANTED: HOLY PRIESTS

Depart! Depart! Go out from there, touch no unclean thing; Go out from the midst of her, be clean, you who bear the vessels of the Lord. (Isa 52:11)

Therefore when Jesus perceived that they were about to come and take Him by force to make Him king, He departed again to the mountain by Himself alone. (John 6:15)

The world had no influence whatsoever on our High Priest. He didn't need men to give Him authority. Publicity and popularity were never His goal. More than once, Jesus warned others not to make Him known (Mat 12:16). The *moonlight*, not the *spotlight*, was the highlight in Jesus' ministry. He spent many nights and early mornings alone in prayer. The mountain was His preference. It was there that He secured the Father's presence. It was there that He made His choices while blocking out other voices. It was there where He was given new manna for each new day. This is where Jesus received His authority. Priests, hearken! If you do not spend time with God *alone,* you will always be a *clone.* You will clone ministry ideas, visions, and strategies from others. You will copy and imitate the gifts and graces of others. Your authority will only come from man. You will drink from someone else's well (anointing). You will steal someone else's word. You will be a spiritual schizophrenic.

Fresh manna every day will result in doing things God's way. Fresh bread bakes in the oven of fresh fellowship. You will always have hot bread (messages) for yourself and to serve the people.

Many of God's priests have not worn their garments well. They have neglected the lot and portion of their lives and ministries, who is the Lord Himself. Instead of the Spirit's incubation giving them fresh

43

revelation, they allow insecurity and intimidation to produce a soulish imitation void of God's power. In making their own plans and choosing their own course, they invite a spirit of *divorce* to come between themselves and the Lord. A glad reunion awaits them, if they would only turn to the Lord with all their hearts. *Intimacy with God is the cure for the imitation of men.* There's a unique holy oil reserved for you alone.

> *And you shall anoint Aaron and his sons, and consecrate them, and they shall minister to Me as priests. And you shall speak to the children of Israel, saying: 'This shall be a holy anointing oil to Me throughout your generations. It shall not be poured on man's flesh; nor shall you make any other like it, according to its composition. It is holy, and it shall be holy to you'. (Ex 30:30-32)*

Priest, bake your own bread. Wear your own garment. Buy your own oil. Draw from your own well. Climb your own mountain.

The travail of your own soul will make your spirit whole. Christ will come to the front. Flesh will move to the back. The quiet retreat of your soul will propel the Spirit's attack. Your soul will *extract* the old and *attract* the new. The stale will move out and the fresh will move in. The Lord will be drawn to your broken, subsiding soul. The light will break forth and all will be clear as the Spirit of the Lord draws near. Wrong steps will be made right as you walk in the light. Shadows will flee in the Holy of Holies. Weeds and thorns are plucked out, and pure seeds will now sprout. It's all in His presence. Rain begins; droughts end; frustration ceases; satisfaction increases - all in His presence.

Alterations are made in His presence. You are refurbished and restored in His presence. You are redesigned and remade in His presence. You advance as you dance in His presence. Expectations are raised as the Lord is praised. Your wounds are healed, and your destiny sealed. Wineskins are renewed, and His words become your food - in His presence. Mishaps are averted, and demons are diverted by His presence. Warnings are given, and life is worth living in His presence. All His loving and all His kissing; you don't know what you've been missing in His presence. Oh, what so many priests lose by neglect - by default - when they fail to show up - when they fail to draw near!

Good corporations and companies are known for their good benefits. Consider the benefits of the King's company: Lifetime opportunity, eternal benefits, eternal security, a sure identity, a great working environment and so much more. Each day every priest only needs a piece of the true Bread from heaven. Priest, get your piece!

> Oh, cry for personal holiness, constant nearness to God by the Blood of the Lamb! Bask in His beams; lie in the arms of His love; be filled with the Spirit; or all success in the ministry will only be to your own everlasting confusion. (Quote from Robert M. McCheyne) (Hill, 1993. p. 71)

LAUNCH OUT

Launch out into the deep...(Lk 5:4)

Shallow waters are the place of being sin or self-conscious and of toiling in your own strength. With many priests the issue no longer is sin but *self*. Self-consciousness is a result of spending most of your time in the inner court. Time and again priests stop short of the Holy of Holies, the place where you are God-conscious. These are the deep waters. Peter's sin and self toil kept him in the shallow waters. Sin and self keep us all close to the shoreline and away from the deep. When, like Peter, we see how wide the gap is between the shallow and the deep, between our futile efforts and God's power and holiness, then there will be a falling down, a humbling of ourselves and a grieving (Lk 5:8). Be of good cheer, for this is the beginning of your transformation. The process of transformation begins with a forsaking of your own strength and a denying of your own self – a yielded-ness and a tender broken-ness. As we will soon see, it took Peter a long time to learn this lesson.

Peter was first introduced to Jesus by Andrew, his brother (John 1:41-42). Peter *came* to Jesus. This was a *casual* encounter. After the miracle of the fish (Lk 5), Peter *followed* Jesus. This was a *convicting* encounter. Peter was convicted of *sin*. But Jesus said he would now catch men. ...*From now on you will catch men.* (Lk 5:10)

Conviction must be present to catch men. Many cities and regions are void of the power to really save. The *deep* waters are the place of power to save. The power has been restricted, and men have not been convicted because demons have not been evicted. Priests have stopped short of the Holy of Holies. They have not given birth to human spirits on the earth. Demons blind men's minds and hold their wills. Inner court priests cannot cast out demons of this kind. It takes a higher kind of faith. Unbelief lingers in the inner court. Prayer and fasting helps take you beyond the veil (Mat 17:21). Beyond the veil, demons are bound and human minds are loosed. Beyond the veil, men's wills are freed, and new human spirits birthed from incorruptible seed. Souls are converted first beyond the veil. Priests, the face of your ministry and the atmosphere in your city can change dramatically beyond the veil.

Part of the reason men *come* to Jesus but don't *follow* Him is a lack of travail keeps them in an infant state. Beyond the veil is travail.

My little children, for whom I travail in birth again until Christ is formed in you. (Gal 4:19)

Oh priest, the people in your city are dying! Oh priest, the Christians in your city are carnal! Death is advancing! Life is restrained! Oh priest, don't you care? Oh priest, how long - how long will you wallow in the shallow waters? How long will you refrain from your priestly responsibilities? How long will you hear the cries of dying

46

men and not respond? How long will you sit idly by and watch the poor being oppressed? Pray now, not later! You're not an administrator, but a mediator! Weep! Don't just sleep! Go on out into the deep!

Watch for things which prevent you from persevering in prayer and defile your priestly role. Watch for sluggishness and shallowness in prayer. The presentation of your ministry office before the people will then be tainted with more of the self nature than the God nature. Lack of depth in prayer usually results in some showmanship in the pulpit. These days there is so much pizzazz on the platform, prosperity in the pocket, and so little power in the pulpit. There's so little burden in the pew because there's such spiritual poverty on the priest. Haughtiness has been so common and brokenness so uncommon.

Lack of true Holy Spirit prayer and brokenness produces a wrong basis for ministry and chokes a priest's pure love for people and pauses the moving of compassion. It results in a *platform* based, *program* based, and *performance* based ministry. The only kind that Jesus knows and approves of is a *people* based ministry. Peter only discovered how big his life could be after the "fish" miracle. Again, Jesus told him he would now catch men. In other words, Peter would have a people based ministry. But Peter had so much yet to learn in the school of Christ.

The pillars of a *people*-based ministry are always heart-felt prayer and passionate evangelism birthed by the Holy Spirit. When it's not, then the unsaved tend to be forgotten and will sometimes end up at the bottom of a minister's mental list (though most would never admit that). Think about it. How many churches are really aggressively making ongoing plans to reach the lost in their communities? There's your answer as to how many churches and ministries are people based. Excuses will always come and say it is too hard. No, the problem is we're too cold. Kingdom work done lawfully is hard work. It's heavy, rigid, and grinding. What's done in love is fulfilling and fluid. Love is the Lord's yoke. The law is man's yoke. Which yoke are you under?

Submit to the Holy Spirit. Go for the spirit of prayer. Ask God to break your heart. Your human nature must give way to the Divine nature. Only then will you have real power to help, heal, and save. Are you looking to reach a new plateau in your life and ministry? Go deeper in self-denial and travail. Ask God for the spirit of grace and supplication.

According to the weight of the burden that grieves us is the cry to God that comes from us (Hill, 1993. p. 12).

Find a burden that *grieves*.

Launch out into the deep (Lk 5:4). Once more, shallow waters are the place of *superficial* ministry which is platform, program, and performance based. Deep waters are the place of *supernatural* Holy Spirit ministry which is people based. It's a place of agonizing prayer and travail. The deep is where the fish are biting. There's power to convict and save men. It's a place where you lose control and God takes control.

THE PRIESTLY PRIVILEGE OF SUFFERING

He went a little farther and fell on His face, and prayed, saying, 'Oh My Father, if it is possible, let this cup pass from Me; nevertheless, not as I will, but as you will.' (Mat 26:39)

Give birth to tenderness. Give birth to weeping. Give birth to the compassion of Jesus. Go into the Holy of Holies. Stand in the place where the Son of man has gone, and feel and be touched with the infirmities of man. Go in there, hard man, and be turned to tenderness. Give place to the things of My Spirit that you've been denied. Time and time again you've come, but you've never gone far enough. Worship Me now and love will transform you (Prophetic utterance).

Suffering servants are so because they're touched with the agony of the infirmed. Suffering servants give birth to spirit. The more you deny yourself and suffer in the flesh according to the will of God, the more authority you gain in the Spirit. This is the law of Christ (based on love) which is also the law of every priest. Actually, the deeper you go in God, the more painful it can be. As you draw nearer to the heart of God, it's only fitting that He not only share His joy with you, but His pain and sorrow as well. *The costly oil that sets men free is the kind that's bought through suffering.* Godly suffering for the sake of the gospel and for others births the glory of God.

So then death is working in us, but life in you. (2 Cor 4:12)

Compare the ministry then and the ministry now, especially as we know it in the free world. We boast in our monuments, our meetings, and our men. Paul boasted of the Messiah, martyrdom, and the marks on his body (Gal 6:17). We boast in our creeds and credentials. Paul boasted in the cross and the crucifixion (Gal 6:14). We boast of being slain in the Spirit. Paul boasted of being stoned in the city. We boast of our programs and prosperity. Paul boasted of persecutions and prisons. Did he know something we don't yet know?

Today most ministries are known for their great preaching, large congregations, books they've written, or countries they've been to. Paul's letter of recommendation was based on the sacrifice and sufferings he had endured to obey God and preach the gospel (2 Cor 6:4-5).

One time a friend of mine preached a message on dying to self, but wondered why there was so little response from the people. His wondering ceased when, after the meeting, he heard the pastor make the following statement: "My people are taught that Jesus has already died, and now all they have to do is live for Him." With such erring philosophies oozing from the mouths of some of today's leaders, is it any wonder why some of these churches have so little power? It's because many of our leaders have never suffered and been totally spent for the sake of Jesus and the gospel. Death has never worked in them, so life is lacking in those they minister to.

> I wonder if one who is unmoved (by this world's suffering) can ever be a servant of the suffering Lord! My brethren, I do not know how any Christian service is to be fruitful if the servant is not primarily baptized in the spirit of a suffering compassion. (Author's parenthesis) (Jowett, 1905. p. 35)

Identification is a primary attribute of the priesthood of God (Heb 5:1-2, 4:15). Identification with the sufferings of humanity births compassion, which then produces an authority to deliver. There is so little true deliverance from sin, sickness, and bondage because there is so little authority that is bought through suffering (Heb 2:18).

I recently heard about an inner city mission to the poor and homeless that trains and equips its workers by sending them out for a few days to live like the homeless people on the streets. They dress in the same scanty and ragged clothing, eat the same food, and sleep where the homeless people sleep. For a few days, their entire manner of life is exactly the same. Needless to say, these gospel laborers return from the streets totally changed, with a new compassion and authority to reach the homeless street people. It is said of William Booth, founder of the Salvation Army that he desired to hang his officers over the fires of hell for a time so that they would go forth into the streets with a greater compassion for the lost. The *will* of man is bent, yielded, and conformed to God's will and learns obedience through identification and suffering.

THE MIXTURE OF WILLS

Not everyone who says to Me, 'Lord, Lord,' shall enter the kingdom of heaven, but he who does the will of My Father in heaven. (Mat 7:21)

50

...he who does the <u>will of God</u> abides forever. (1 John 2:17)

Entrance into the kingdom of heaven is dependent on doing the will of the Father. This must be every believer's aim. In your will lies the power to *do* and to *act*. True holiness is reflected in the life of a person who wills not to sin against God in thought, word, *motive*, and deed.

It is the delight of every holy priest to do the will of the Father (Ps 40:8). In fact, it is their meat as it was the meat of our Master (John 4:34). Doing the will of the Father gave Jesus nourishment and satisfaction. When a person is not nourished and satisfied in his spirit, he will try and find that satisfaction in his flesh or mind with selfish desires. And the desires of a man are tied into his will. Selfish desires are evidence that you are doing your own will.

Any desire to save your life is a false desire (Mk 8:35). The devil and our flesh are constantly trying to feed us with false desires, desires to save our lives and not lose them. Again, your desires will always join forces with your will. The way to change your desires is to change your will. It is man's will which gives access to selfish and evil desires dominating his life. It is also man's will which gives access to holy and godly desires. The will of man is one of the most powerful forces on the earth. *The safeguard against doing your own will and being forever deceived is to always be feeding your will with desires to lose your life and not save it.*

For I have come down from heaven, not to do My own will, but the will of Him who sent Me. (John 6:38)

Jesus craved the Father's will like a starving man craves food. Do you crave God's will this way? Do you desire it more than physical food? Do you have a deep longing for complete obedience to the will of God, or are you satisfied with partial obedience? Think about this: No amount of desire existed in Jesus for things, relationships, or experiences outside of the Father's will. He received and gave His strength and energy only to the Father's will for His life, whether it

51

was hard or easy. Many say they want God's will for their lives until there's a measure of hardship and suffering in it. The love for God will desire His will, but it is the fear of God that bends the human will to obey God even through hardship and suffering.

One place where many people miss God is when God's will leads them into a difficult place. Unwillingness to endure hardship and difficulty according to the will of God can be a manifestation of impure motives. It can mean you've attached conditions to obeying God. As long as the journey is fairly easy, many will continue to obey God, but they have reservations about going too far. If you keep resisting places of hardship, challenge, and trial, you will be stunted in your spiritual growth. If you break the cocoon of a caterpillar during the process of metamorphosis, it will never become a butterfly.

The ministers who were denied entrance into the kingdom of heaven in Mat 7:21 were greatly deceived. Their words (they called Jesus, Lord), and their works (they prophesied, cast out demons, and performed miracles) apparently were not properly aligned with the will of God. How can this be since people were helped and set free by these miracles and deliverances? You see, these so-called ministers did not draw their strength and energy from seeing people helped, but from their lust for power and fame. They were false prophets (Mat 7:15) whose lust for power made them strangers to the Lordship of Jesus.

False prophets will be everywhere in these last days. They will deceive many with their words and even works because they are religious. Religion fools many people because there is scripture and often, even power attached to it. *False prophets are so deceptive because they use the scriptures to do their own will.* Their desire is to save their life and get their gain. But those who remain close to the heart of God will know they are false. Not even their sheep's clothing will deceive those who are true believers. They will discern the inward lack of brokenness and humility in these false prophets, and will instead detect the cry of the ravenous wolf (Mat 7:15).

We are known and judged in heaven more by the fruit of our lives than the fruit of our ministries (No matter how many people are helped by the gifts and power in our ministry). Both Samson in the Old Testament and Judas in the New Testament worked miracles, but both of them stand today as the ultimate example of what it means to have a divided heart and a double life. If genuine love for God and for people is not attached to our ministries, then we are on dangerous ground. The real fruit of our ministries is only a by-product of the fruit of our lives. And our message is the link between our life and our ministry. Prophets and priests, hearken! If we preach (message) what we do not practice (life), we are *master* hypocrites (Jam 3:1).

One of the biggest problems in the Church today is self-appointed, self-made, and self-willed priests. In Jeremiah's day it was the same. *"And the priests rule by their own power..."* (Jer 5:31). The devil is not God's greatest enemy. He's been defeated by our Lord Jesus Christ. Neither is he the greatest force of evil. The human self will is the ultimate source and force of all evil. It is the will which gives the flesh and the devil access to control and rule any life. The human self-will, which is often mixed with religion, reasoning, and a sense of righteousness, is the most deadly and dangerous. It can breathe, live, and move in the church without ever being exposed. It can disguise itself in the church with proud achievements and perfect attendance. It can talk about the cross without ever getting on it. It can boast in Jesus without ever making Him Lord.

One old man who was miraculously used of God often instructed believers to wait before the Lord until there were no longer two wills involved in any matter they were seeking Him about. Wait long enough until the only will that remains is the will of the Father. God abhors mixtures of His will and man's will. God will be glorified among those who approach Him. The desire of every true priest must be to lose his life for the sake of Jesus and the gospel (Mk 8:35). That is the place where his will is aligned with God's will. Conversely, when a priest's desire is bent toward saving his life, the will becomes contaminated with an unholy mixture.

Priests (bishops) must not be "self-willed" (Tit 1:7). When they are, it extinguishes their ability to judge and rightly discern between the secular and the sacred, the soul and the spirit. Jesus could hear and judge, and His judgment was just because He did not seek His own will (John 5:30). In other words, He was accurate in everything He said and did, because He continually yielded His own will to the will of the Father. Priests and all believers whose hearts are truly yielded to the will of God, even if that will involves hardship and some suffering, are much more sensitive to the leading of the Holy Spirit than those who are not fully yielded. Those with pure motives have a much greater grace to see, hear, and properly discern God and His voice. They walk before the Lord with fear and trembling. Holy fire burns in the altar of their hearts.

A fire shall always be burning on the altar; it shall never go out. (Lev 6:13)

This was a literal altar, but the altar of every New Testament priest is now in his heart. That is where true holiness is found. This is to be the beauty of every priest. *Is the altar of your heart burning with holy fire or is it filled with cold ashes?*

God wants holy priests. It is time to make an exchange; your cold ashes for the beauty of His holiness.

Any takers?

Chapter Six
THE HURT THAT HEALS

So Peter went out and wept bitterly. (Lk 22:62)

During the miracle of the fishes Peter felt the pain of his sinful life and separation from God (Lk 5:8). The real significance of that miracle is that it accused Peter of his mediocre life in comparison to the power of a holy God. Before God soundly saves a man He thoroughly convicts him. It has also been said that before God uses a man greatly He hurts him deeply. There's a hurt that's holy. *There's a hurt that heals.*

As human beings God will grieve us and hurt us, if you will, so His healing can be released. Permanent "heals" come from deep hurts. Sure joys come from deep sorrows. The power of His resurrection comes from the fellowship of His sufferings. If you're grieving for whatever reason, even if it's for yourself (like Peter), you are closer to God than you may think. You're closer to the Lord than most happy people. Happy people are shallow because happiness is based on circumstances. Joyful people are deep because joy is based on the Lord. And the Lord was a man acquainted with grief and sorrow.

Think of Peter for a moment. He had been in ministry with Jesus for more than three years, but his base and focus was still off. Although he had left everything to be in ministry, his basis was still platform, position, and performance based. Peter was convicted of *sin* at the beginning, but now he was convicted of *self*. The sword went deeper this time. It was a bitter blow that cut to the core of his nature.

There's a little Peter in all of us. His words were great; his actions were often heroic; but his *motives* were always in question. Hidden for some time, pressure finally revealed what was in his heart. In a day where we are taught to believe and to speak great things about ourselves, we need a fresh revelation of how deceptive our self-nature can be. Peter was always bold and fearless when he was with the "team" (the apostles and Jesus). Alone, he denied Jesus. Under pressure, he bent; he bowed. How could he have denied the One he loved? It's real simple. *Peter denied Jesus because he did not deny himself.* His basis for ministry was position and performance. It was self based, not love based.

Wasn't it Peter who struck the servant of the high priest's ear in the presence of a multitude with swords and clubs (Mat 26:51-55)? What a fearless act! What a bold performance! How could this same man deny Jesus in the presence of a servant girl? And let's not forget that Peter wasn't the only one who boasted of his allegiance to Jesus. All the disciples did (Mat 26:35). And when the pressure was on, the disciples also forsook Jesus and fled (v 56).

In the presence of his "teammates" Peter *performed*, but in the presence of a servant girl he became *deformed*. He changed colors. One moment he was *red* with retaliation and seeming boldness. But the next moment he was *yellow* with timidity. He acted like a "rock", but he was still a "reed". His hand was strong with the sword, but his heart was weak. With the Lord, "hand" service is one thing, but "heart" service is what He wants. In the garden Peter slept. Then later he wept. In the garden he failed to prepare for the coming storm, so his house was shaken. It would result in the death of a promise, not the Lord's, but Peter's.

These turn of events at the end of Jesus' earthly ministry were not necessarily the best way for Peter to learn about himself. Remember, it was the devil's plan to sift Peter. However, the scriptures and history tell us that in most cases, unless some men utterly fail, they will not be broken and humbled. The earlier sword used by Peter to cut a man's ear was now cutting his heart. It wasn't the servant's ear that needed breaking, but Peter's heart.

The servant's ear would only hurt for a moment, but Peter's heart would hurt for a few more nights. The servant's ear would be healed immediately (by Jesus), but Peter's healing would be delayed. He boasted of his *dying*, but Jesus spoke of his *denying*. In the act of his denial, those words of Jesus would bitterly wound Peter. The servant's pain was only skin deep. Peter's pain pierced his heart. He would finally see himself for who he really was. Then he would be changed.

The Word comforts and encourages us, but it also corrects and rebukes. Actually, there are two things which can hurt us for our good; the Word of God and suffering for the sake of righteousness. Tests and trials play a part in making us partakers of His holiness (Heb 12:7-14). Chastening through these two means is painful, but perfecting. It hurts, but it heals. I've heard theologians and Bible teachers say that it's only the Word that chastises us. "Tests and trials come because we're in a fallen world that's ruled by the devil, and God doesn't need the devil to perfect us in holiness," they'll say. But wait a minute. Do not the scriptures say that the Word of God tries us (Ps 105:19)? Without tests and trials, how then can the Word try us? How can we prove the Word of God without going through a time of testing? How can there be victory in the Word without a battle in the world? How can we really know what is in our hearts without pressure being applied to it? I understand that it is the Word alone that searches and tries the deepest thoughts and intents of our hearts (Heb 4:12), but it still takes pressure, persecutions, tests, and trials to prove that Word in your life and remove the impurities. The removal of these impurities, however, is still done through our faith and obedience to the Word of God during the tests and trials. Do you see it? It still comes down to proving your obedience to the Word and the will of God for your life. And you cannot prove anything without a test.

The Word of God exposes us and also tries us. Allow me to give you examples of these operations. The face and foundation of my wife's life was changed violently and dramatically through a painful encounter she had with the holiness of God via the proclamation of the Word.

One night in a meeting, an altar call was made for people to get right with God. There were many ministers in attendance. Only my wife responded at first until another person joined her. The Holy Spirit used the message preached that night to convict her of being position and platform based in her desire to minister. She was feeling a bit of self-pity for being overlooked among other missionaries. The Spirit exposed the ugliness in her heart. The darkness she saw made her cry. Ministry had become an idol. She, with only one other person, went to the altar and repented, as many ministers watched. She smashed her idol and made Jesus the Lord of her ministry life. Her spirit *cried* and then *revived*. Self disappeared, but God reappeared. Up until that time, her spiritual life had been a desert. In a very short few days, the heavens would open.

Days passed and my wife prayed again, but this time in a different manner. After attending a real miracle crusade where she witnessed the wonderful power of God, a desire rose up in her heart. At this time in our lives we were missionaries in West Africa ministering in a Muslim nation, and we had not yet seen any significant breakthroughs. With a sincere desire to reach the Muslims with the gospel, my wife prayed for this anointing which was present in this crusade. Three or so days after, a fresh new wind of the Spirit came on her life in the area of prayer. As her husband, I can testify that she has been totally different ever since. When her motives were truly aligned with God's heart, her fellowship was renewed. The Lord honored her request.

To this day the presence of God remains on her in a tangible way in prayer, worship, and intercession. It is certain that if she had continued on in ministry operating under false motives while still seeking God for His perfect will, severe tests and trials would have been necessary to prove the Word of God in her life and to remove the impurities that were in her heart. Of course, all this could only happen with her cooperation and through her faith in the Word of God.

At times God may try you by putting His finger on the most tender places of your life. Personally, it was my desire to marry before ever going to Africa as a missionary. I had literal dreams that I'd marry this particular girl whom I had been courting. When it didn't happen, I felt hurt and discouraged. In my immaturity, I blamed God for the disappointment. Unanswered questions bred doubt and distrust in me. Why did God allow these dreams of marrying this girl? How could I trust the Lord again? Would my heart respond to the Lord and to ministry with the same zeal again? And how could I ever move on to the next phase of my life and calling? Only the answers to these questions would bring freedom to my life once more. In my desperation, I cried out to God. He heard me and answered me.

Shortly thereafter the word of the Lord came to me through a prophet of God. This man did not know me or my situation. He ministered to me supernaturally and said that the dreams of marrying this girl were all a test, and that God wanted to know if I'd still serve Him. When the word of the Lord came through this prophet, he pointed at me and I fell backwards and began to laugh uncontrollably. I was totally set free to serve God again. Peace and trust were restored.

You see, at one time I had said in my heart that I would not go forth to the mission field until I was first married. Although this is a legitimate, God-given desire, God was requiring of me in this instance to surrender that right. God will not deal with all of us the same way, but our love for the Lord will be tested. With some it may not be a matter of a spouse, but perhaps the desire for an education or a career or a particular lifestyle.

Pure love flows only from a pure heart. A pure heart is like pure gold, which can only be purged from alloys and mixtures and made pure when it is tried in the fire. Our faith becomes purer when we let patience have its perfect work in life's fiery trials. Joseph's attitude in the pit and the prison made all the difference in the world. Impatience and bitterness would have stopped God from eventually promoting Joseph. The same was true of David. His patience and steadfastness in the wilderness while being hunted down by Saul proved, purged, and profited him. It was a pain that purged. It was persecution that profited. It was a hurt that healed. It prepared David for his future as king.

Men that keep choosing God despite all their tests, trials, pain, and persecution are men whom God can trust because their hearts have been proven. Their love is pure. Pure love is based on choice. Even Jesus learned obedience by those things which He suffered (Heb 5:8). In other words, the Son of God had to learn to make right choices. Remember, it is in our suffering that we really learn obedience and allow our love for the Lord to mature (John 15:14).

God tests us to know what is in our hearts (Deut 8:2). And He will touch the dearest and most precious things in our lives to do it. One of the greatest examples of this in Scripture is when God asked Abraham to offer up his son Isaac. But doesn't God already know what is in our hearts? Didn't God already know that Abraham would obey? Yes, but it still must be proven. Covenant is not in word only, but in deed. But God will go even deeper than just deeds and touch us in our hidden motives. *You can be approved by men for your words and deeds, but disapproved by God for your motives.*

As I said before, sanctification is a process that begins at new birth, but should continue throughout our lives. The process of sanctification is when the Holy Spirit will take our lives and begin conforming them to Christ. At new birth we are new creations in our spirits, but as newborn babes in Christ, we must then mature. Babies are perfect, but not mature. It's not a question of increased righteousness, for all the righteousness a true believer has is in Christ. We can never add to our righteousness either now, in this present life, or throughout eternity. Our faith in Christ alone supplies all the righteousness of God we will ever need. A believer can never add one iota to the righteousness of Christ. We are already accepted and complete in Him (Col 2:10). However, when we are born again we do not overcome the pride of life, the lust of the flesh, and the lust of the eyes completely. There is a pruning and a purging which the believer must yield to in order to produce more fruit (John 15:2). Although we cannot add to our righteousness, we can increase in the fruits of righteousness (Phil 1:11).

Cultivation must be deep for much fruit to abound. The sword of the Spirit must probe our motives from top to bottom. The deeper the *tilling,* the richer will be the *filling.* God will not purge you without your consent. That's why Christians can live and die with so little true fruit to show for their labor. They were not *willing* for a deeper *tilling.* A heavenly plowing is always brutal. It deals with the inner self. It prepares the heart for a heavenly planting which will produce a heavenly harvest.

Joseph was given a dream of being a ruler (Gen 37:5-11), but from the time of the dream to its fulfillment there was a pit and a prison prepared for Joseph to endure. These fiery trials were necessary to purge Joseph from false motives and selfish ambition. The Word of the Lord tested him through these trials (Ps 105:19).

As another example, Peter initially was not willing to face the persecution of being identified with Christ (Lk 22). Therefore, he was sifted. As it turned out, even in his denial, because he was sorrowful and repentant, he would be pruned and purged, and the motives of his heart refined. The lack of preparation through prayer in the garden caused Peter to faint in the trial. It was Jesus' praying that caused Peter's faith not to totally fail (Lk 22:32).

Furthermore, we have had human fathers who corrected us, and we paid them respect. Shall we not much more readily be in subjection to the Father of spirits and live? For they indeed for a few days chastened us as seemed best to them, but He for our profit, that we may be partakers of His holiness. Now no chastening seems to be joyful for the present, but painful; nevertheless, afterward it yields the peaceable

fruit of righteousness to those who have been trained by it.
(Heb 12:9-11)

Partaking of pain is necessary to produce partakers of holiness. Pain doesn't feel good, but it "*hurts good.*" The Father corrects and chastises us for our profit. Don't run from it, but subject yourself to it that you may live and yield the fruit of righteousness.

THE SECOND CIRCUMCISION

At that time the Lord said to Joshua, 'Make flint knives for yourself, and circumcise the sons of Israel again the second time.' (Jos 5:2)

And the Lord your God will circumcise your heart and the heart of your descendants, to love the Lord your God with all your heart and with all your soul, that you may live. (Deut 30:6)

For he is not a Jew who is one outwardly, nor is circumcision that which is outward in the flesh; but he is a Jew who is one inwardly; and circumcision is that of the heart, in the Spirit, not in the letter; whose praise is not from men but from God. (Rom 2:28-29)

The practice of circumcision had been halted in Israel for one whole generation, obvious signs of the nation's disobedience and apathy. In this age of grace, circumcision is not of the flesh but of the heart. When apathy creeps into our lives we need a second circumcision. Apathy is a vital sign of a lack of life in any church or Christian. It is one of the telltale symptoms of a dying church and a backslidden believer. As spiritual physicians, ministers must not treat the symptoms, but the cause of apathy.

Before I list some wonderful qualities of a circumcised heart, let me give you some alarming symptoms that will help you in detecting apathy. Are you ready for a serious heart check? Okay, take your defenses down. Apathy is setting in when:

- An hour in prayer seems so long, but so short when watching a good movie.
- It is laborious to read a chapter in the Bible, but easy to read 200 pages of a best-selling novel.
- Gossiping about someone is easier than sharing the gospel.
- We can't fit a gospel meeting into our schedule with a yearly planner, but we can schedule other events at a moment's notice.
- We scramble to get a front seat at a ball game, but are content to sit in the back row of a church meeting.
- We get thrilled because a football game goes into overtime, but complain because an inspired sermon is too long.
- A ten dollar bill looks big in the offering, but small at the market or mall.

Idolatry leads to apathy. Any motivation of the heart having to do with selfish gain is idolatry. Idolatry begins when you start giving your heart's affections to someone or something more than God. In this state, a second circumcision is necessary to restore the heart to its supremacy of loving God above all else.

Sin's roots lie not in your words or even your deeds, but in the motives of your heart. In one form or another, all selfishness is sin and a sign of immaturity. Let's compare some characteristics of selfishness that lead to apathy, proof of an uncircumcised heart in certain areas, with the characteristics of a circumcised heart. Again, let's go through these with an open heart and with the hope that it will expose our blind spots, birth godly repentance, and then lasting change. Check carefully the areas of your life that are manifesting selfishness:

- Selfish people desire to be served, but a circumcised heart is motivated to serve others.
- Selfish people desire to be a success, but a circumcised heart is motivated to make others a success.
- Selfish people desire personal advancement at the expense of others, while a circumcised heart desires to advance and

promote others.

• Selfish people have a drive to be recognized and appreciated, but a circumcised heart has a sense of its own unworthiness outside of Christ and is just grateful that God would use it at all.

• Selfish people are wounded when others are promoted and they themselves are overlooked, but a circumcised heart is eager for others to get the credit and rejoices when others are lifted up.

• Selfish people think of how much they can do for God, but a circumcised heart knows they have nothing to offer outside of Christ and His life flowing through their broken lives.

• Selfish people feel confident in how much they know, but a circumcised heart is humbled by how much it doesn't know and has yet to learn.

• Selfish people are self-conscious, while a circumcised heart is not concerned at all with self.

• Selfish people are self-righteous and look down at others, but a circumcised heart esteems others better than itself.

• Selfish people have an independent, self-sufficient spirit, but a circumcised heart has a dependent spirit and recognizes its need for others.

• Selfish people are self-protective of their time, their rights, and their reputation, while a circumcised heart is self-denying.

• Selfish people claim their rights and have a demanding spirit, but a circumcised heart yields its rights and has a meek spirit.

• Selfish people focus on the failure of others, but a circumcised heart is overwhelmed with a sense of its own need.

• Selfish people possess a critical, fault-finding spirit and are always trying to remove the speck out of someone else's eye, while a circumcised heart is merciful and forgiving and is busy removing the beam from its own eye.

• Selfish people find it difficult to share their spiritual needs with others, but a circumcised heart is willing to be open and transparent with others as God directs.

• Selfish people work to protect their reputation and self-image and are overly concerned with what others think, but a circumcised heart is willing to die to its own reputation and to what others think. Its only concern is being real with God.

• Selfish people are defensive when criticized, but a circumcised heart receives criticism with a humble and teachable spirit.

• Selfish people are quick to blame others and make excuses, while a circumcised heart accepts personal responsibility and can see where it is wrong.

• Selfish people do not wish to be vulnerable, but a circumcised heart is willing to get close to others and risk vulnerability.

• Selfish people are blind to their true condition and don't think they have anything to repent of, while a circumcised heart walks in the light, and realizes its need for a continual attitude of repentance.

• Selfish people want to always cover up their sin and make sure no one finds out, but a circumcised heart doesn't care who knows or who finds out as long as God is pleased.

• Selfish people have a hard time admitting wrong and asking for forgiveness, but a circumcised heart is quick to admit failure and seek forgiveness.

• Selfish people deal only with general confession of sin, but a circumcised heart is willing to acknowledge specifics when confessing its sin.

• Selfish people are concerned only about the consequences of their sin, while a circumcised heart is grieved over the root cause of their sin and of the hurt it brings to the heart of God.

• Selfish people are only sorry they got caught or found out in their sin, but a circumcised heart is genuinely sorry for its sin and proves it by forsaking it.

• Selfish people wait for the other person to come and ask forgiveness when there is a conflict or a misunderstanding in a relationship, but a circumcised heart runs to the cross no matter who is wrong, taking the initiative for reconciliation when there are conflicts or misunderstandings.

• Selfish people compare themselves to others and feel superior or inferior to them, but a circumcised heart compares itself to the holiness of God and feels a desperate need for His mercy and grace.

• Selfish people don't think they need a second circumcision but are sure everyone else does, while a circumcised heart continually senses its need for a fresh encounter with God and for a fresh infilling of the Holy Spirit.

Apathy is defined as a lack of feeling or emotion. It also means indifference. Over a period of time, selfishness will lead to apathy. When apathy has set in and your love has waxed cold, you need a serious second heart circumcision. Through the power of the blood of Jesus and of the Spirit of God, you can have a resurrection of godly desires, if you will repent and forsake your own will and selfish desires. This is what I call a second circumcision. This is true revival in the heart of man, which is initially birthed through true repentance.

Besides all of the characteristics listed above, the circumcised heart has four basic distinct qualities:

1) A fervent love for Jesus.
2) A holy hatred for sin.
3) A pure love and good will toward man.
4) A heart cry for revival and lost souls.

If you study past revivals and those of today, you will discover these qualities in the people who are affected by the Holy Spirit in revivals.

These qualities should not be thought of as rare, but normal.

What kind of heart, then, does the Spirit of God circumcise and revive? Are there certain qualities that God looks for? The following scriptures reveal the heart to which God is drawn.

> *Thus says the Lord: 'Heaven is My throne, and earth is My footstool. Where is the house that you will build Me? And where is the place of My rest? For all those things My hand has made, and all those things exist,' says the Lord. 'But on this one will I look: <u>On him who is poor and of a contrite spirit, and who trembles at My Word.</u>'* (Isa 66:1-2)

> *For thus says the High and Lofty One who inhabits eternity, whose name is Holy: I dwell in the high and holy place, with him who has a contrite and humble spirit, <u>to revive the spirit of the humble, and to revive the heart of the contrite ones</u>.* (Isa 57:15)

God looks *to* and lives *with* the humble and contrite heart that trembles at His Word. This is the way to experience personal revival. Keep on humbling yourself. Impress God. Be attractive. Peter's bitter weeping (Lk 22:62) attracted the Lord. "*But go, tell His disciples and Peter...*" (Mk 16:7). After the resurrection, the Lord remembered Peter and singled him out. He was forgiven. Peter's bitter weeping gave way to sweet rejoicing. He hurt, but then he healed. His contrite spirit was revived. Deep repentance always means deep revival. A second circumcision is for restoring your first love (Rev 2:4).

Has your love waxed cold? Have you left Jesus? Has apathy crowded Him out? For your return He still waits.

Inhabiting eternity is not enough. Jesus wants your humble heart.

Chapter Seven
THE MASTER ON MOTIVES

In the parable of the two sons (Mat 21:28-32) who were commanded by their father to work in the vineyard, one son *said* he would *not* go, but then went. The other son *said* he would go, but then did not. Among other things, this short parable taught by Jesus proves that words are not as important as *deeds*. We are commanded to love, not in word or in tongue, but in deed and in truth (1 John 3:18). Words void of works are oftentimes dead. In studying the life and ministry of Jesus, I found that it was not His habit to voice His love for others, but to show it. No matter what our initial intentions may be, if they do not culminate into obedience, they mean nothing.

In the parable of the goats and the sheep (Mat 25:31-46), the judgment on the goats was severe, but the point is clear. It's what you do, not just what you say that counts. The Lord doesn't know many who call Him Lord (Mat 7:21-23). But the judgments of Jehovah go even deeper than deeds.

Many years ago when I was in Bible school, a female classmate of mine, while in prayer one day, developed a sensitive burden for other fellow classmates. It had been her observation that many of them were rather discouraged. So one glad morning my friend decided to stand at the door of the classroom and hand each student a pamphlet on the joy of the Lord.

Ignorant of school policy, which prohibited student solicitation of any literature, my friend's actions were wrong. She got in trouble. Her penalty was very severe; in fact, too severe for me. The dean called her into his office, took her school I.D. badge, and expelled her from classes for several days. Irate and feeling like unrighteous judgment had been poured on my friend's head, I rushed to her aid. In the dean's office and to his face, I explained to him why he erred in his judgment of my friend. Although according to school policy her actions appeared wrong, her heart was right in this matter.

Deeds at times may appear wrong even when the heart is right. And the same holds true in the reverse, when deeds, by mere appearance may look right, but are disapproved by God because the heart is wrong. We are admonished to love in deed and in truth. *It's not just what you do that's important, but what you do in truth.* How often we deceive others and ourselves by our pretentious words and deeds! How often we misjudge others and ourselves by the same!

The dean specialized in doing things right, but in this case, he didn't do the right thing. He judged my friend by his book, but God judges us by *The* Book.

> *You shall love the Lord your God with all your heart, with all your soul, and with all your mind. This is the first and great commandment. And the second is like it: You shall love your neighbor as yourself. On these two commandments hang all the Law and the Prophets.* (Mat 22:37-40)

> *Therefore, whatever you want men to do to you, do also to them, for this is the Law and the Prophets.* (Mat 7:12)

The Law is based on *deeds*. The Prophets are based on *motives*. "What you do for others" are deeds; "as you would want them to do for you" are motives. Deeds appear on the surface, but motives run deep. Deeds done in truth are deeds done with a right heart and right motives. A truthful person is a person true in motive. It's not just what you do, but *what you are* that is clearly known in heaven's book of remembrance.

Under the law unregenerate men could only judge themselves and others by deeds. They needed prophets anointed with the Spirit to deal with men's hearts. John the Baptist preached and commanded the people to bear fruit or deeds worthy of repentance (Lk 3:8). He asked for fruit, but the problem was in the *root*. Under conviction the people asked John what they should *do* (deeds) (Lk 3:10, 12, 14). Although the above commandments deal with the heart, under the shadow of the Law heart matters were not clear. Jesus, ministering as The Prophet still under the dispensation of the Law, would redefine the commandments and introduce a clearer way. Under the Light of Jesus and His teachings, the motive of the heart would now be laid naked.

The Sermon on the Mount set the stage and the standard for the clearer laws of the kingdom. Let's look at The Law and The Prophets and briefly break down the teachings of Jesus in Mat 5, 6, and 7:

- The Law denounced murder. The Prophet denounced anger (Mat 5:21-22).
- The Law commanded gifts be brought to the altar. The Prophet rejected the gift when reconciliation of a brother was wanting (Mat 5:23-24).
- The Law denounced physical adultery. The Prophet denounced the look (deed) to lust (motive), which is adultery in the heart (Mat 5:27-28).
- The Law dealt with the hand and the touch. The Prophet prescribed a self-denial of such (Mat 5:29-30).
- The Law pardoned a certain divorce. The Prophet pointed to hardness of heart (Mat 5:31-32; 19:9) as the reason for this course.
- The teachers of the Law swore by an oath. The Prophet said, "Let your word, not your oath, be your anchor of truth." Truthful people don't need to take oaths. The motive for taking an oath is to appear truthful even if you lie (Mat 5:33-37).
- The teachers of the Law promoted retaliation in every case. The Prophet urged good in evil's face (Mat 5:38-42).
- The teachers of the Law justified hatred of its enemies.

71

The Prophet called for loving them (Mat 5:43-47).
- The Law focused on perfect deeds; the Prophet on perfect hearts (Mat 5:48).

Matthew 5, 6, and 7 mark the distinct beginning of a great new age. The Sermon on the Mount marked the dawning of a new order in God's kingdom. This message, one of Jesus' first sermons, was the *Masterpiece*. Literally, it was the piece missing from the Law. It cut to the core of man's heart and laid bare his true motives.

In Matthew 6 Jesus speaks of three areas where hypocrisy seems to be most evident: giving, praying, and fasting. Isn't it interesting that in the greatest areas of potential for power, where the kingdom of God makes its greatest advances, is where the greatest potential for hypocrisy also exists? Hypocrisy has its roots in the desire to please men or to be *seen by men* (v 1-2, 5, 16). If you treasure the glory and smile of men more than the glory and smile of God, then you are laying up treasures on the earth (Mat 6:19-21). This is a form of the fear of man. The fear of man keeps your heart bound to earthly values and earthly honor. When you derive your authority from men's praise, then man is your master.

The more you value the praise of men or fear their disapproval, the greater your motivation will be toward pleasing men more than pleasing God. Its root is a lust for power, approval, and success in the eyes of man. Coveting power, approval, and success over purity of heart and service will birth deception. Falsehood will creep in. Truth will slip out. Righteous judgment will become blurred. Your eye will be bad, and the light in you will be great darkness (Mat 6:23-24). You could eventually become prey for punishment (Mat 25:46).

The quickest way to become a goat (Mat 25:31-46) is to covet anything more than purity of heart and purity of service. True security is found only in purity of heart and purity of service. Giving, praying, and fasting are great works of light that become darkness when the motive is to be seen by men. But here again is the amazing thing: Giving, praying, and fasting are all the will of the Father. Outwardly these acts appear to be great in sacrifice and self-denial. Isn't it interesting that, even in doing these things, the heart can be so corrupted? It's not only doing the will of the Father contained in these acts that matters, but doing it from a purity of heart. That is what gets His reward. The only safeguard that I have found against impure motives is to desire the secret place, as Jesus said (Mat 6:6), more than the public place. *Acts of self-denial are always defiled when done for man's smile.*

When Jesus came on the scene the spiritual climate was filled with dense fog. There was very little light. The atmosphere was one of great hypocrisy. I believe there are three kinds of spiritual atmospheres that are predominant in Christendom: hypocrisy, hype, and true holiness. Hypocrisy is found in greatest measure in religious settings where there is form but little fire. A hypocrite is one who play-acts and imitates. Hype, on the other hand, is a false excitement or a false fire. It is smoke with no substance. It is a shout with no clout. But true holiness frees us from both hype and hypocrisy, which often run together.

Hypocrisy is the deception, but hype is like the fruit of deception. A hypocrite is a deceived person who cannot discern between an atmosphere of hype and true holiness. Remember, without holiness no man can see the Lord. Holiness is the character of God. Holiness is an honest and transparent heart.

When you are more concerned with the smile of men than you are the smile of God, you cannot be honest with yourself. You will cover and conceal your true self because of your desire to impress and please men. This is a subtle form of hypocrisy. Being different publicly than what you are privately places a veil over your eyes. Real change begins privately. Real change begins on the inside, not the outside.

Who you are when nobody is looking is who you really are.

Chapter Eight
WHEN THE NARROW BECOMES BROAD

In the days of Noah only a few souls believed the word of the Lord and were saved from an earth-destroying flood. Of all the people God delivered from Egypt, twenty years old and upward, God said only two would enter the land of promise (Numb 32:11-12). Out of 32,000 of Gideon's men only 300 qualified and passed God's test to be chosen to deliver Israel (Jud 7). One of every four who hear the Word of God ever produce fruit (Mk 4), and approximately 8 of 100 bring forth one hundred fold fruit. One hundred twenty disciples out of the multitudes Jesus ministered to were waiting for the promise of the Holy Spirit (Acts 1, 2). And a few in a Christian church in the city of Sardis were undefiled and worthy to walk with Jesus (Rev 3). Jesus said narrow is the gate and difficult is the way which leads to life (Mat 7:14). Why do we attempt to make it broad and easy?

Sanctification begins but does not end with salvation. Its pursuit is lifelong. Not only is the entrance into eternal life narrow (not based on works, but on the finished work of Christ), but the Christian Spirit-led walk is also narrow, confined, and with hardships. As a matter of fact, the further you go on with God, the narrower it gets in the natural realm, and the less options you have, but the broader it becomes spiritually as your heart is enlarged. There are few who enter the narrow gate, but there are even fewer who walk in power because there are few, who after salvation, continue to choose the narrow way.

Then one said to Him, 'Lord, are there <u>few</u> who are saved?' And He said to them, Strive to enter through the narrow gate, for <u>many</u>, I say to you, will <u>seek</u> <u>to</u> <u>enter</u> and will not be able. (Lk 13:23-24)

Jesus is the only way. He is the narrow gate. The admittance price was paid with His Blood. Passage is obtained by repentance and faith.

And according to Jesus, *many* will seek entrance but *won't be able* to pass through. Bible teachers will often say that this text is written with only the Jews in mind, but it is a scriptural principle.

A rich young ruler came to Jesus and asked the same question.

Now as he was going out on the road, one came <u>running</u>, <u>knelt</u> before Him, and <u>asked</u> Him, 'Good Teacher, what shall I do that I may inherit eternal life?' (Mk 10:17)

This man was an earnest inquirer. His running and kneeling before Jesus shows that he is not casual but desperate. Although he said he'd kept the commandments, there was one thing he lacked.

Then Jesus, looking at him, <u>loved</u> him, and said to him, "<u>One thing you lack</u>: Go your way, sell whatever you have and give to the poor, and you will have treasure in heaven; and come, take up the cross, and follow Me" (21).

The response Jesus gave to this man seems severe but it was God's love in operation. The root of all evil is the love of money, and this was the man's problem. So deep was this root that it called for a severe sword to extract it from the young man's life. What Jesus ministered to this man was both grace and truth. The truth was stern and strong, but it came with grace. Jesus looked at him and loved him. What a Savior! His grace wished for the man's obedience to this word so he could inherit eternal life, but His truth would keep Jesus from any sort of compromise and from administering a false comfort. Faithful are the wounds of a friend (Pr 27:6) and open is the rebuke of a true lover (Pr 27:5). And the friend and lover is the Lord.

Grace and truth await restoration in the church. The definition of grace has been *milky* and truth has been *watered down*. Grace and truth will forever coexist. Jesus is both (John 1:14). The real glory of God, who is Jesus, must have as its ingredients, grace and truth. Grace without truth will mislead and deceive. Similarly, truth without grace will condemn and kill. But grace and truth together will save and deliver. When Jesus often spoke gracious words, the people would marvel (Lk 4:22), but the truth would sometimes fill those same people with wrath (Lk 4:23-28).

The prescription Jesus administered to this rich ruler may have seemed like a bitter pill to swallow, but it was the only way, the narrow way. The bitterness would have turned sweet once it got in the man's belly (heart). A freedom he had never yet known, even with all his riches, would have been his. You see, the seemingly sour medicine Jesus gave this man was for one reason: to deliver him from the bondage of greed and covetousness. It was to set him free from the love of money and his trust in uncertain riches. It was so Jesus could truly become Lord of his life, and he could inherit eternal life. Anything less than the prescription Jesus gave would have allowed the man to enter the kingdom while still serving other gods. And this can never be.

This word made the rich young ruler sad and sorrowful (v 22). If preachers are not making people sad, mad, or glad, then God hasn't sent them. The problem today is we don't have enough *narrow-minded* preachers. *Broad-minded preachers are paving the way for the destruction of many.* It's not through works that men are saved, but through repentance and faith (Acts 20:21). The rich young ruler did not repent of serving his "wealth" god, and instead of trusting in God, he continued to trust in riches. It was all a heart issue. Salvation is of the heart. "But doesn't the Bible also say that to believe and call on the Name of the Lord is all that's needed to be saved?" (Rom 10:9) You're missing the whole point. It's what happens in the heart that matters. It's like this: If a man has sexual relations with his wife, does that mean she's pregnant? Of course not. Other conditions must exist for conception to take place. The womb must be open, and the sperm and egg must germinate for life to begin. The same is true spiritually. It takes both the Word and the Spirit working in a man's heart for genuine conversion to occur. It takes both repentance and faith to seal a person's salvation. When it comes to the basic doctrine of salvation, we have fallen short of the glory of God. We've had milky grace and watered down truth. And faith has often been preached without repentance.

One can believe and be convinced of the power and reality of Christ and Christianity, and even be baptized, and still be poisoned and bound by very selfish motives in becoming a professing Christian. Simon the sorcerer was such a one (Acts 8). He believed and was baptized, but the condition of his heart leaves us room to doubt where he really stood with God. When he saw the power of the Holy Spirit in operation, Simon offered money to possess this same power, not only for personal use, but to be able to give it to others (Acts 8:19). You see, before Simon's profession of faith, he had a name and a reputation around the city as some great power of God (v 9-11). He astonished people with his practice of witchcraft and sorcery. Now that he'd seen the real power of God, he was making bids on it. But Peter sharply rebuked him and called him to account.

> *You have neither part nor portion in this matter, for your heart is not right in the sight of God. Repent therefore of this your wickedness, and pray God if perhaps the thought of your heart may be forgiven you. For I see that you are poisoned by bitterness and bound by iniquity.* (Acts 8:21-23)

In this superficial age of "covered up" truth, we probably wouldn't have been so stern and strong with old Simon. We may have even gotten a kick out of his desire for power. We may have even laughed and chuckled about it. But the naked truth was that Simon's heart was not right with God. He believed Philip's preaching and was baptized, but now he needed to repent. Peter didn't smile on this supposed little innocent baby Christian. Instead, he thundered with apostolic authority, "Your money perish with you, because you thought that the gift of God could be purchased with money!" (v 20)

Salvation is of the Lord and it is God who grants repentance (2 Tim 2:25), but He gives both grace and space to repent (Rev 2:21). With men salvation is impossible, but with God it is possible (Mk 10:27). However, He will never compromise the truth and make the narrow gate broad and the hard way easy (hard on the flesh).

Then Jesus looked around and said to His disciples, 'How <u>hard</u> it is for those who have riches to enter the kingdom of God.' (Mk 10:23)

Note the disciples' astonishment at Jesus' words (v 24). Then Jesus reiterates and expounds on the difficulty of entrance the rich man will have into the kingdom of God. Now watch the reaction of the disciples.

And they were <u>greatly</u> <u>astonished</u> saying among themselves, 'Who then can be saved?' (Mk 10:26)

The disciples went from being astonished to being *greatly* astonished. Listen to A.W. Tozer's revealing words:

> We serve a God today who very rarely ever astonishes anybody. He manages to stay pretty much within the constitution. Never does He break over our bylaws. He's a very well behaved God and very denominational and very much one of us, and we ask Him to help us when we're in trouble and watch over us when we're asleep. The God of the pretentious believer isn't a God I could have much respect for. But when the Holy Ghost shows us God as He is, we admire Him to the point of wonder and delight.
>
> There are a great many bogus Christs among us these days. John Owen, the old Puritan, warned people in his day: 'You have an imaginary Christ, and if you are satisfied with an imaginary Christ, you must be satisfied with an imaginary salvation.'
>
> There is only one Christ, and the truly saved man has an attachment to Christ that is intellectual in that he knows

79

who Christ is theologically. For you, there is the romantic Christ of the female novelist, and there is the sentimental Christ of the half-converted cowboy, and there is the philosophical Christ of the academic egghead, and there is the cozy Christ of the effeminate poet and there is the muscular Christ of the all-American halfback. But there is only one Christ, and God has said that He is His Son. (Tozer, 1969. p. 24)

Therefore consider the goodness and severity of God; on those who fell, severity; but toward you, goodness, if you continue in His goodness. Otherwise you also will be cut off. (Rom 11:22)

Many love to know and hear about the Lord's goodness and mercy, and how He forgives sin. Many love to quote the scripture where Jesus told Peter that if a brother sinned against him seventy times seven (that's 490) times in one day and repents, that he should forgive him (Mat 18:21-22). Somehow, to the insincere believer, these kind of scriptures work to give him some kind of leverage or license to continue living loosely and following the dictates of his carnal desires. This person's image of God is that He exhorts but never exposes, restores but never rebukes, comforts but never confronts.

> Many love to know His kindness, but very few are willing to know His severity. If you do not embrace both, you will always be in danger of deception and of a fall from His great grace. You must remember both His kindness and severity if you are to stay on the path of life. The true love of God includes the judgment of God. You must know the Lord's kindness and severity or you will fall to deception. (Rick Joyner, 1996. p. 76, 121)

To presume something to be true about God that is not true is one of man's great transgressions. It is idolatry. It changes the glory of God into an image. It leads to a false service of a false God based on a system of false beliefs. An incorrect understanding of God's true

80

nature has probably damned more human beings than anything else.

Of course, God is good and merciful. And yes, His love is unconditional. Anyone who has been truly forgiven and changed by God's power knows this. If somehow you are among those who only see God as a strict disciplinarian or a hard taskmaster, consider how His unconditional love is displayed every day. Let's pretend and imagine God's love to be conditional by asking a series of "what if" questions:

- What if God couldn't take the time to bless us today because we didn't take the time to thank Him yesterday?
- What if God decided to stop leading us tomorrow because we didn't follow Him today?
- What if God would not hear us today because we failed to listen to Him yesterday?
- What if God answered our prayers the way we answer His call to service?
- What if God met our needs the way we give Him our lives?
- What if God stopped loving and caring for us because we failed to love and care for others?
- What if God refused to give us any more sunshine because we grumbled when He sent the rain?
- What if God took away the Bible tomorrow because we would not read it today?

Of course, God's love is unconditional! Of course, He is good and merciful! But He is also just and sometimes severe. Emphasizing God's justice without balancing it with His mercy results in legalism. People will then begin to serve God only out of guilt, an unwholesome fear, and duty. On the other hand, a lack of emphasis on the severity of God and His judgments can cause great apathy among Christians. They soon forget that it is a fearful thing to fall into the hands of the living God (Heb 10:28). It is in beholding the severity of God and His judgments that a wholesome fear of God is birthed in our hearts. And it is the fear of God that causes a departure from sin. Is it any wonder why there's been so much sin, carnality, and apathy in the Church? The root cause of all of it is idolatry. And the cure for idolatry is a correct and balanced understanding of the true nature of God.

The narrow becomes broad when God is misinterpreted, when His image becomes blurred, when His character is misconstrued.

The narrow becomes broad when God's severity is mistaken for cruelty, when His goodness is confused with leniency and permissiveness.

Enter the narrow gate. Walk the difficult (confined) way. Listen to Jesus! His words are life.

Chapter Nine
MOTIVES AND VALUES

The lamp of the body is the eye. If therefore your eye is single (clear), your whole body will be full of light. But if your eye is bad (selfish), your whole body will be full of darkness. If therefore the light that is in you is darkness, how great is that darkness. No one can serve two masters; for either he will hate the one and love the other, or else he will be loyal to the one and despise the other. You cannot serve God and mammon (riches). (Mat 6:22-24 NAS) (Additions from Moffatt's translation.)

Where is your treasure? What do you esteem and value in life? Where do your strongest energies flow? What is it in you that releases joy and passion? Therein lies the focus of your life. Therein lies the treasure of your heart (Mat 6:21).

If you were in a desert dying of thirst, water would be your treasure. If you were attempting to gain passageway into a foreign country, your passport with visa would be your treasure. Where the light of eternity is valued and esteemed, there is Christ, the greatest and most precious treasure.

Two people can sit in the same seat and hear the same word of God time after time. One succeeds, and the other fails. Two criminals were crucified with Jesus. One believed, and the other mocked. One saw the Light because his eye was single and clear. The other criminal's eye was bad or selfish (Moffatt's translation), so he did not *value* or esteem Christ even in his dying hours.

The word "value" is an important word. It means to regard highly, to rate according to relative worth or desirability, to appraise or esteem. The word is used several times in the New Testament. Jesus used it to tell the disciples of their value in comparison to birds (Mat 6:26, 10:31), and of a man's value in comparison to sheep (Mat 12:12).

83

Listen now to these powerful words and understand why the word "value" is so important. What you value most in life is what you will pursue. The more you value Christ, the greater your motive is to please Him. *The invisible powers of Light and darkness know that the greatest value in life and in death is the person of Christ.* The moment a human being discovers the real value of Christ, he will follow after Him. The moment any person discovers the real value of Christ is also the moment when darkness and worldliness begin to lose their grip on that life.

> *And this I pray, that your love may abound still more and more in knowledge and all discernment, that you may approve the things that are <u>excellent</u>, that you may be <u>sincere</u> and without offense till the day of Christ. (Phil 1:9-10)*

The word "excellent" in the above scripture is the same word as "value" in the comparison Jesus makes to men being of more value than birds or sheep (Mat 6:26; 10:31; 12:12). Part of the apostle Paul's prayer for these Philippian believers was that they would "surely learn to sense what is vital, and approve and prize what is excellent and of *real value*, recognizing the highest and the best, and distinguishing the moral differences..." (Phil 1:10a Amp).

In our lives, consciously or unconsciously, we place priority on those things we value. God wants us to be able to recognize and distinguish between temporal and eternal values. Many believers place too much priority on earthly values and the world's value system of success and failure. The will of God is what has the highest and the best value in both this life and the life to come.

What has priority in your life right now is what you value. Jesus taught that whatever you value above Him disqualifies you from being His disciple (Lk 14:26-27, 33). He stated emphatically that you are not even worthy of Him if you place more value on human relationships than on a relationship with Him.

So many Christians live life on such a shallow, superficial basis because they do not prize and esteem things that are excellent and of real eternal value. It is the will of the Father to reverse every Christian's earthly appetite and value system.

One time I was ministering to a group of teenagers, and as always, among them were spiritually hungry ones, and others who simply had little appetite for God. In this particular meeting there was one young man who stood out to me. He was dull in spirit and oppressed. During the praise and worship part of the service, he didn't sing or raise his hands, or render any kind of response throughout the entire meeting. But that afternoon in a basketball game, this same young man was running up and down the court shouting and competing with such intensity. I thought, "Is this the same guy that was in the meeting this morning?" His energy and appetite was passionate toward basketball, but numb toward God. His value system needed alteration.

God's will is for every believer's love to abound so much that it creates an approval and esteem in his heart for the things which are excellent and of real value. This will result in transparently pure and sincere lives which will bring no offense or opportunity for you or anyone to stumble (Phil 1:9-10). *Your values determine your motives, and right motives are what keep you pure and free of offense.*

Kingdom values are not based on religious activities, but on love for God and people. Jesus' disciples were busy traveling and ministering with Jesus, but they forbade little children from coming to Him (Mk 10:13), tried to keep blind Bartimeus from crying out to Jesus for help (Mk 10:48), and attempted to send the hungry multitudes away (Mat 14:15). They didn't consider the value of even one soul (Lk 15:1-10). The discovery of the actual value of the kingdom of God must exert a master influence over our lives to the effect that we love Jesus more than anything else, and the value of a soul is esteemed above any earthly and temporal blessing.

SINCERITY OF HEART

...That you may be <u>sincere</u> and without offense till the day of Christ... (Phil 1:10b)

Grace be with all those who love our Lord Jesus Christ in <u>sincerity</u>. Amen. (Eph 6:24)

...If therefore your eye is clear (<u>single</u>, as the KJV has it), your whole body will be full of light. (Mat 6:22)

The word "single" as in "if your eye is single" (Mat 6:22), and the word "sincere" (as in Phil 1:10 and Eph 6:24) have similar meanings. Lock these two definitions in your spirit:

> *Single*: Without dissimulation or self-seeking; clear; without guile or duplicity; singleness of purpose which keeps us from the snare of having a double treasure and consequently a divided heart; sincere.

> *Sincere/Sincerity:* The unleavened bread of *sincerity* and truth as in 1 Cor 5:8 is *eilikrineia* in the Greek, which literally means "judged by sunlight". The word alludes to Oriental bazaars where pottery was displayed in dimly lit rooms. Unscrupulous merchants would patch cracked pottery or cover defects with wax. Intelligent buyers would hold up the pottery to the sun and judge its quality by the sunlight. *Eilikrineia* is transparent honesty, genuine purity, manifested clarity, and unsullied innocence. It describes one who does not fear thorough examination of his motives and intents, because he has nothing to hide. (Word Wealth, p.1725, The Spirit-Filled Life Bible, Thomas Nelson NKJ, 1991)

The single eye and the sincere heart is one of the most important components of the entire Christian life. In the same way the light

86

that the eye receives guides the body, the light that the heart or spirit receives guides your life. Duplicity means darkness. Singleness means sight. Only the pure in heart have an anointing to interpret, discern, and see God (Mat 5:8). Without holiness no man can see God or what He's doing. Jesus was accurate in seeing, hearing, and judging because He did not seek His own will, but the will of the Father (John 5:30). Because His value was the will of the Father, Jesus' motives remained pure throughout His life and ministry. His heart was never divided. He remained free from any spot or blemish to such a degree as to bear examination in the full splendor of the sun. Because Jesus never sought His own will but always the Father's will, He had understanding by which one is able to see all things intelligibly and clearly, and proceed without mistake.

When we substitute earthly values for eternal values it hinders our discernment and ability to see. It aborts our understanding and dims our ability to interpret and judge. It sets us up for deception.

What we see with our eyes is always colored by the condition of our hearts. "Unto the pure all things are pure" (Tit 1:15). A fuss was made in a meeting one time when a woman who was slain in the Spirit remained on the floor with her leg and dress up in the air. But it didn't bother the pure in heart, whose focus was on what God was doing. *We see things not as they are, but as we are.* That's why a double-minded man receives nothing from the Lord (Jam 1:6-8). His heart's loyalty is divided. One cannot trust such a man because his eye is cloudy, his decisiveness vacillates, and his judgment is uncertain.

In the remaining verses of Matthew 6, Jesus expounds on the dangers of worry and covetousness, and thus, a divided heart. He warns his disciples concerning the cares of this life, and tells them to seek the kingdom and not things (Mat 6:33). Most genuine Christians will guard their hearts against immorality, uncleanness, or some other outward sin, but how many would consider guarding their hearts from the cares of this life? Actually, one of the greatest signs of the last days and the return of Jesus is that people will be caught up in the cares of this life (earthly values) and in making a living (Lk 17:26-30). All of these instructions were for the purpose of keeping their hearts pure, and their eye single.

The church at Laodicea was counseled by the Lord to anoint their eyes with eye salve so that they might *see* (Rev 3:18). The believers in this church thought they were rich and in need of nothing, but the Lord said they were wretched, miserable, poor, blind, and naked (v 17). They could not see or discern their true condition. They were serving mammon (materialism) and not God. Their value system had become warped. Their eye was bad (selfish), their vision was cloudy, and their perspective was tainted by a covetous heart. They were guilty of trying to do what Jesus said cannot be done, and that is, serve two masters.

The anointing for the Laodicean believers to see (discernment), and the white raiment to cover their nakedness (true righteousness) could only be given as their motives were refined by the fire of tests and trials. This is the reason the first counsel Jesus gave them was to *"buy from Me gold refined in the fire..."* (Rev 3:18). A heart can only be found pure after it's been tested and tried like pure gold. The only way to refine gold is to purge it of its alloys and impurities by trying it in the fire. Since their hearts were found lacking in purity and sincerity, these believers needed to buy gold (faith) tried in the fire. Jesus commanded them to be zealous and repent (v 19). To remain pure, our faith must always be tested and tried. *"That the genuineness of your faith, being much more precious than gold that perishes, though it is tested by fire, may be found to praise, honor, and glory at the revelation of Jesus Christ"* (1 Pet 1:7). Remember, our eyes are colored by the condition of our hearts. The heart of the church at Laodicea was lacking in genuine faith and it rendered them naked, and impaired their ability to see.

Our motives are at the depth of who we really are. Often our own hearts can deceive us and lead us astray. That is why tests and trials are necessary - because they reveal to us what is in our hearts.

We can justify our every deed but God looks at our motives. (Pr 21:2 LB)
All the ways of a man are pure in his own eyes, but the Lord weighs the spirits---the thoughts and intents of the heart. (Pr 16:2 AMP)

There was a mighty intercessor that lived in the first part of the nineteenth century whom God dealt with to take a Nazarite vow. This meant among other things that he could not cut his hair nor shave. God put him through this test in order to refine the deepest motives of his heart. It was a fierce battle since in those days respectability was even more revered than it is today. This intercessor and his family were greatly respected in their church and in their town. When this man's hair began to grow, people began to wonder if he'd lost his mind. Rumors spread all throughout the church and the town. This man's family bore much of the reproach. And yet the most challenging thing about this whole endeavor was that this intercessor was not allowed to explain to anyone why he was doing this. For me personally, that might have been the most difficult part of it all. But you see, God wanted his servant to get victory over the fear and opinions of man. Obedience here came at a high price. This choice servant of God was learning that pleasing God is to be valued above pleasing man.

> *Bondservants, be obedient to those who are your masters according to the flesh, with fear and trembling, in sincerity of heart, as to Christ; not with eyeservice, as menpleasers, but as bondservants of Christ, doing the will of God from the heart, with goodwill doing service, as to the Lord and not to men.* (Eph 6:5-7)

At times severe tests are not even necessary to perceive what is in a person's heart. Oftentimes our motives can be easily seen by our actions in the daily routine affairs of life. For instance, when I was a young man in Bible school I was offered a job on campus. There were a few fellow Christian classmates I worked with who I found out were man pleasers and time servers. When the supervisor was not around, they were slothful, but whenever the supervisor showed up, everyone got busy and became more diligent with their work. I could never understand these students' concept of Christianity. I mean it is one thing to act like that in the world, but in the kingdom? I was so grateful just for the convenience of working right there at the Bible school. I can't say that I was always the perfect employee, but I had a tender conscience when it came to working "as unto the Lord." Who cares if the supervisor is there or not? The Lord is there. One brother even got angry with me one time because everyone else stopped working early at the end of the night to clean up, but I always tried to work right up until the last minute. I was just following my convictions with fear and trembling, in sincerity of heart, working as unto the Lord.

You see, it's the fear of God that produces a single eye and sincerity of heart. The fear of God is what helps to cleanse you of every fleshly deed and false motive. The fear of God is what keeps you free from the fear and intimidation of man. It is the cleansing agent that keeps your heart pure. It keeps your conduct and conversation as unto the Lord and not men. It is in the fear of God that holiness is perfected (2 Cor 7:1).

The rich young ruler claimed to have kept the commandments (Mk 10:17-22), but he could not esteem Christ above his riches. He was bound by earthly values. But Moses esteemed even the reproach of Christ greater riches than the treasures in Egypt (Heb 11:26). Where your treasure is, there your heart will be also (Mat 6:21).

If treasure is hidden in a field, and you are not willing to sell everything you have to buy that field, then your heart is not fully in the treasure (Mat 13:44). If you're not willing to sell everything and follow Christ, then the kingdom of heaven is not yet ruling your heart. You may only be a professing Christian. Your eye is bad. Your life is self-centered. The light you claim to have is darkness. The narrow way you claim to be on is broad. You can fool people with your words and deeds, but you face God now and on judgment day with your motives.

For we must all appear and <u>be</u> <u>revealed</u> <u>as</u> <u>we</u> <u>are</u> before the judgment seat of Christ, so that each one may receive [his pay] according to what he has done in the body, whether good or evil, [considering what his purpose and <u>motive</u> have been, and what he has achieved, been busy with and given himself and his attention to accomplishing]. (2 Cor 5:10 AMP)

On that day, your motives will reveal only the real. *Don't wait until then to find out who you really are.*

Chapter Ten
THE HEAL THAT HURTS

A certain ministry advertisement promoting its meetings caught my attention with these somewhat questionable claims:

> "Come and experience the blessings of God! Be strengthened by hearing the deep truths of God's Word, which will lift every believer from defeat to victory and power. You will learn the secrets of the triumphant Christian life by receiving teaching on such subjects as healing, financial prosperity, deliverance, hope, and protection. You will never be the same!"

Now please do not misunderstand me; there's absolutely nothing wrong with the listed subjects above. We believe in all the blessings of God, and we want to encourage people to receive them and walk in them. But let's not exaggerate the truth. Let's not take that which amounts to the minor truths of God's Word and make unscriptural claims about how these are the "deep truths," and the "secrets of the triumphant Christian life." There always exists a great danger when we put an overemphasis on any scriptural truth, but more so when it's a minor truth. Are there not vital organs in our physical body that we must have to survive which are more necessary than others?

For example, let's take the area of financial prosperity. Financial prosperity is certainly not wrong. God desires for His people to prosper, and maybe some ministries are called to teach it (although to emphasize it leaves me in doubt), but financial prosperity is not the *heart* of the gospel nor is it a principle doctrine of the New Testament. At best, it is only a benefit of it. Yet you couldn't tell it today because many preachers have put such an overemphasis on it.

What about healing? I believe God's will is for every sick person to be healed. Jesus bore not only our sins but our sicknesses and diseases on Calvary (Mat 8:17). Healing is scriptural and God's plan is divine health for each of us. That is a part of our covenant. Additionally, all believers should be exercising their rights in laying hands on the sick (Mk 16:18), and some ministries are called to minister specifically in this area, but healing is not the *brain* of the New Testament. However, when one is sick, healing is the best gift they can receive at that time because that is what they need.

I believe if more Christians would simply walk in obedience and seek first the kingdom of God all these blessings would be theirs to enjoy (Mat 6:33). Perhaps that is where the emphasis needs to be. While I do strongly believe that the gospels and the book of Acts largely promote healing, signs, and wonders for suffering, hurting, unsaved humanity, Paul and the other writers of the New Testament simply do not give much content to the subject of healing for Christians.

But for many believers, these minor truths and the pursuit of the blessings of God are the biggest part of their diet. The desire for material blessings, riches, and the pleasures of this world encompasses virtually their entire Christian experience. I find it quite ironic that the devil has somehow used the blessings of God and financial prosperity acquired through supposed "faith in the Word" to actually steal the Word from believers' hearts. Such is the deceitfulness of riches and the lust for other things. If the pursuit of comfort and convenience, wealth, and happiness is our primary motivation, we will always be deceived and disapproved.

For whoever <u>desires</u> to save his life will lose it, but whoever loses his life for My sake and the gospel's will save it. (Mk 8:35)

If your desire or motive for riches, blessings, and things is to save your life, to preserve it in order to become safer and more secure, then you are no longer obeying the gospel of the Lord Jesus Christ. How then can the above ministry advertisement make such claims that a series of teachings, which amount to learning to appropriate God's blessings in our lives, somehow make us extraordinary, triumphant Christians? It's somehow portrayed as the ultimate teaching which will defeat the devil, the world, and the flesh in our lives, and bring us complete victory.

Is your motive to really serve and glorify God or is it to satisfy and gratify self? That is the rock solid criteria for judging every action. Speaking of rock, when I was first saved I loved my rock and roll music. I thought it was okay to continue to listen to the Beatles, Aerosmith, and the Rolling Stones, but my big brother in the Lord straightened me out. Very frankly he spoke to me and told me that anything which does not glorify the Lord is sin. "Does this music you're listening to glorify God, or does it gratify self?" he asked. The same criterion applies to the blessings of God, or even what we would call innocent amusements and past times, of which sports, recreation, and entertainment would be the biggest part.

Charles Finney, the great revivalist of the eighteenth century, received a lot of flak and opposition for a series of articles he published and sermons he preached on the subject of Innocent Amusements. Finney came down hard on ministers who focused their time on devising more ways to amuse and entertain the youth. Finney preached strong against squandering precious time and unnecessarily spending the Lord's money. He even said that eating and drinking was sinful if done merely to gratify the flesh (1 Cor 10:31). Finney believed and taught that every intelligent act of a moral agent is right or wrong, innocent or sinful. Listen to his criteria for judging whether such acts are innocent or sinful:

> Nothing is innocent unless it proceeds from supreme love to God and equal love to man, unless the supreme and ultimate motive is to please and honor God. In other words, to be innocent, any amusement must be engaged in because it is believed to be, at the time, most pleasing to God. It must be intended to be a service rendered to Him---a service which, on the whole, will honor Him

more than anything else that we can engage in for the time being. I take this to be self-evident. (Finney, 1996. p. 92)

In Finney's day, much like today, he felt that many Christians were acting under a great delusion because they believed there was nothing wrong or sinful about harmless amusements, sports, and entertainment. Again Finney writes:

> When speaking of amusements, they say, 'what harm is there in them?' In answering to themselves and others this question, they do not penetrate to the bottom of it. If on the surface they see nothing contrary to morality, they judge that the amusement is innocent. They fail to look for the supreme and ultimate motive, which will tell them if the act is innocent or sinful. But apart from the motive, no course of action is either innocent or sinful, any more than the motions of a machine or the acts of a mere animal are innocent or sinful. No act or course of action should, therefore, be judged innocent or sinful without determining the supreme motive of the person who acts. (Finney, 1996. p. 95-96)

But, some would argue, "Hasn't God given us all good things to enjoy? Isn't there a danger of falling into legalism and bondage with this type of teaching? What's wrong with watching a good ball game or a clean movie? Or going fishing or sailing? Many have gotten off into 'ultra-holiness' with this kind of extreme teaching. We need balance in life. You need to be careful." But that was the same thing they told Finney, but he never bought it. He kept on preaching, and to this day, he may be one of the greatest recent revivalists this world has ever known. Did he know something we don't?

To whom are these types of teachings a bondage? Whom do they disturb? Is it not those who are pleasure-seeking and entertainment-loving people? Finney did not say that these things were wrong or sinful in themselves. Neither do the scriptures teach such things. There are times when hard working Christians and ministers need to kick back and enjoy some forms of rest and relaxation. There are seasons when participation in certain recreational activities is called for. Actually, in my own life, I find that in the long run, such seasons actually add to my overall productivity, fruitfulness, and health of mind and body. But the motive is what we must question. In many instances it's really a matter of conscience. Richard Baxter provides us with a good rule of thumb:

> Recreation to a minister must be as whetting is with the mower---that is, to be used only as far as is necessary for his work. May a physician in plague-time take any more relaxation or recreation than is necessary for his life, when so many are expecting his help in a case of life and death? Will you stand by and see sinners gasping under the pangs of death, and say: 'God doth not require me to make myself a drudge to save them?' Is this the voice of ministerial and Christian compassion or rather of sensual laziness and diabolical cruelty? (Quote by Richard Baxter) (Bounds, 1972. p. 1)

Some may need more relaxation and recreation than others. How much is too much? Only you know. There are Christians and even ministers who live for such times. Many have lost the fervent heart they once had for God and passion for winning souls. Their motive is no longer to glorify God, but to gratify self. Some Christians work so hard, sometimes working more than one job, so they can have a bigger house, a nicer car, be able to travel more and enjoy life to a greater degree, and provide a good education for their children so they can have the same (again, none of these things being wrong in themselves). Oh yes, we build all these things around going to church, having regular devotions of Bible reading and prayer (in prayer we may tell God how hard we're working, and quote some promise of how He would bless the diligent), and even supporting our missionaries and being involved in doing good deeds (all noble things). To many, however, this is all a delusion, and all these supposed good things actually do is add to and thicken our deception.

A desire for only the blessings and benefits of Christianity without a fullness of heart devotion to Jesus is the subtlest form of idolatry. Is Jesus your ultimate joy and love? Are you running after Him? Is He the longing of your heart?

Beware that you do not forget the Lord your God by not keeping His commandments, His judgments, and His statutes which I command you today, lest when you have eaten and are full, and have built beautiful houses and dwell in them; and when your herds and your flocks multiply, and your silver and your gold are multiplied, and all you have is multiplied; when your heart is lifted up, and you forget the Lord your God... (Deut 8:11-14)

Yes, it's true; the blessings of God can lift up your heart in pride and actually stunt fruitfulness. The cares of this life, the deceitfulness of riches, and the lust for other things choke your fruit (Mk 4:19). Many times the more blessings, riches, and possessions you have, the more care, concern, and covetousness you also have with them. Your heart begins to drift and your desire for these things becomes stronger than your desire for God. You begin going through the outward motions of Christianity without a true love for God.

The devil is an expert at using the things of this world, even the legitimate love for life itself, to turn our hearts' affections toward the earth. Then we begin serving God because we *have to* or because we know it is right instead of a real *want to*. We hear the Word of God on a regular basis but it stops producing in our lives. And sometimes in this state, the more we hear the Word, the harder and more calloused our hearts become. Preachers are sometimes mesmerized because of the lack of fruitfulness in the people they minister to. They need to take heed to Jeremiah's admonition:

Break up your fallow ground, and do not sow among thorns. (Jer 4:3)

Persecution and tribulation from outside make many stumble (Mk 4:18). In the parable of the sower these are called stones. But those things that grow up from inside (cares of life, deceitfulness of riches, and lust for other things), and at first are hidden, will choke us. These are called thorns. If the anointed Word of God is not producing a lasting fruitfulness in the hearers, you better check the ground. It may be fallow. Fallow ground is ground that was once cultivated but is now a wasteland. Weeds choke seeds. Many preachers are sowing seeds when they should be pulling weeds.

Here's a good test for the heart. If it's no longer exciting to worship God and win souls, then thorns have begun to grow in the garden of your heart. Those thorns need to be scorched by the fire of God. The fallow ground needs to be broken up. The "heals" in your life have hurt you. Your heart needs to be circumcised again. The foreskin needs to be taken away (Jer 4:4).

If you've allowed weeds to grow in the garden of your heart and to choke your supreme love for Jesus, then allow the Spirit of God to circumcise your heart again. It may hurt, but in the end it will heal.

Better to have the hurt now that leads to healing than to have the healing now that ends in hurt.

Chapter Eleven
TRUE OR FALSE

He who speaks from himself seeks his own glory; but He who is seeking the glory of the one who sent Him, He is <u>true</u>... (John 7:18 NAS)

...there is nothing <u>false</u> about him. (John 7:18 NIV)

MOTIVES AND MINISTRY

With one eye on his sermon, and one eye on the old wise minister sitting in the first row, the young minister strove to produce a good impression on his older and wiser friend. Once the evangelistic meeting was over, he quickly walked up to the aged minister, and with an apparent air of self congratulation and subtle pride, not to mention a feeling of having preached really well, he asked how he fared. The aged minister fired a sweeping retort that proved very valuable, although at the time disheartening, to the young preacher. "How many people came to the Lord?" the aged minister asked. The lesson was as obvious as the answer to the question. None were saved that night. The young man's falsehood was exposed. He was more interested in his sermon than his subjects. He was more interested in how he fared than how many were saved. He was seeking his own glory rather than the glory of the One who sent him.

A young group of Bible school students left the seminar frustrated because their desire to hear the deeper truths of the Bible expounded by the old prophet of God seemed to be denied. They just didn't understand why the old, experienced man of God didn't delve deeper into the Word of God. "Maybe he's just getting too old to preach," they thought. "Or maybe he's just not studying and praying as much as he should." But the truth was that the older minister purposefully made himself look less intelligent and "lacking depth" to the public eye so that the simple in attendance that evening could understand him. The old prophet of God was more interested in relating to his audience than receiving applause. He was more interested in appealing to his needy subjects rather than appeasing his greedy fans. His teaching originated from God and not from himself. He was true.

Any word spoken or act done in falsehood, no matter how acclaimed it is by public opinion, will not receive honor from God. You may wonder why I use so many ministry examples. It is not to expose, bring suspicion, or breed mistrust concerning ministers. Neither is it to cause you to doubt every minister that comes down the pike. Thank God there are many honest, pure-hearted, and upright ministers still in the land. As a matter of fact, I believe the number of them is growing. Only God alone knows the true motives of every man's heart. Every individual must examine his own heart. Every minister must search his own motives. There's no need to look for something that's not there, either. You can't keep tormenting yourself and doubting every single thing you or others do. However, we must also understand that the most deceiving words and acts are those covered and cloaked with the name of the Lord, and done under the guise of ministry or charity. Jesus and the New Testament writers warned of false prophets and false teachers. People often only know ministers by the visible fruit of their ministries, but God knows us by the fruit of our *lives*. Again, we are known and will be judged more by the fruit of our lives than by the fruit of our ministries (Mat 7:20, 22). The latter is only an outflow of the former. What is more important to you, being successful in public or being successful in private?

I have often wondered in my own ministry how much merit I will receive for all the words and works I've said and done in the name of Jesus. It has caused me to reflect on how much has really been accomplished purely for the glory and honor of God and out of a genuine love for the people. You could say I've done a lot of reflecting, and a lot of repenting. Our own hearts can so easily deceive us if we're not careful.

Allow me to use myself as an example to show how utterly wicked and deceptive our own hearts can be. It happened on the mission field one night during an evangelistic campaign when I was praying for the sick. We were at the close of a meeting in which I had supposedly ministered with all my "heart." There was perspiration running down my forehead and neck. My clothes were drenched. But I was somewhat aggravated because there were no major visible healings or mighty miracles that night. So I laid my complaint before the Lord and told Him that I felt humiliated. "I boasted to the people of Your healing power, and You did not confirm Your Word with signs and wonders!" I exclaimed. After ranting and raving in this manner for a little while I managed to get quiet enough to hear a thought, posed as a question, rise up inside of me. "Why was it so important to you for those people to be healed tonight?" I recognized this question as being from the Lord so I did not immediately respond, but thought on the answer I would give. The Lord wanted me to be completely honest with myself and with Him.

I faced this question head on. It just so happened that on this night we had some visiting pastors from America in attendance, and I wanted so badly to have a good showing. I mean, they had to know that I was a miracle worker, and that God was using me mightily on the mission field. But the darkness gets even thicker than that. I thought perhaps a good showing tonight would also warrant a little extra financial support from these visiting pastors. How dark and deadly our motives become in our quest to be recognized and applauded! How deceitful the heart can be! I didn't care about those sick people, several of whom were blind and crippled. I was more concerned about my own reputation and increased financial support. I had supposedly left houses, lands, and family to be on the mission field, but I hadn't left "self" yet. What a revelation that was to me!

There was another instance where God let me see that what's done in the closet (privacy) of our Christian lives is what is more safely guarded from any falsehood or pretension. The truest test of our character is what we do in private when there are no accolades to be gained. One day at work, long before I ever entered the ministry, I was out in a little park during lunch break having a sack lunch. I was sitting there enjoying the sunshine, when a poor hungry man walked up to me and asked me for one of my sandwiches. In my flesh I really didn't want to share it with him because I was very hungry myself, but the love of God constrained me. I gave him the sandwich and then told him who the real Giver (Jesus) is. The joy of the Lord filled me, letting me know how much this tiny little sacrifice done in total privacy pleased the Lord. It was a pure act done for no reason at all except out of a love for Jesus and that poor man. It is for such pure deeds that we receive praise from God. The Bible calls that pure and undefiled religion (Jam 1:27).

MOTIVES AND MONEY

Money has always been a sensitive subject. In my Christian life I have seen both sides of the spectrum concerning philosophies people have about money. On one side, there are those who will fight to stay poor, believing that somehow poverty equates to holy living and is therefore a real blessing from God. On the other side, there are those who will fight to be rich, considering it to be one of the great pinnacles of godliness. The Bible teaches that both of these positions are extreme. It is not my purpose in this section of the book to get into the theology of money, but into the heart of it. After all, it is not money that is evil, but the love of it.

My wife Carolyn, to whom God often speaks in dreams, was cautioned by the Lord about a wind of doctrine concerning money. The Lord showed her how many believers would suffer as a result of yielding to this wind.

In the dream, both she and I were gathered with a multitude of other Christians at a pool party. People were climbing up on this long rope ladder onto a diving board and then jumping into this huge pool of refreshing waters. Everyone was laughing and having a great time. As people were going up to the diving board on this rope ladder, the wind would blow and sway the ladder back and forth. Because of this wind, Carolyn was hesitant to climb up. You see, Carolyn had her purse with money in it, and didn't know what to do with it. She needed to have both hands completely free to go up to the diving board. Finally, she hid her purse in a gutter on top of the roof of a small building. But then suddenly, as she was walking toward the ladder, that same wind came with such force that it blew many of the people right off the rope ladder and into some high telephone wires. Then, after being burnt, they fell into the water, as the other Christians around them rushed to their aid, and began ministering to them.

The dream is a prophetic warning. Its meaning is plain. There is a wind of doctrine concerning money in which some Christians will be caught up in and for which they will suffer hurt. The refreshing waters represent the fact that the Holy Spirit initiated this move of God, but it got off. Judgment came to many because they did not heed the Lord's warning. Be careful of money. Many ministers have become money-minded and lost the anointing. The problem is not with being rich, but rather, not being rich toward God (Lk 12:21).

Many ministers, including myself, have often said, "You can't do anything without money. It takes money to preach the gospel." This is obvious, but where is the emphasis and what is the Biblical pattern? One time I was so disturbed by the overemphasis on the teaching of financial prosperity that I began to search and seek to see if God had a pattern. Was there to be an emphasis on financial prosperity, and if so, where was the emphasis supposed to be? It didn't take me long to find the answer in the beginnings of the Church age.

Now all who believed were together and had all things in common, and sold their possessions and goods, and divided them among all, as anyone had need. (Acts 2:44-45)

Nor was there anyone among them who lacked; for all who were possessors of lands and houses sold them, and brought the proceeds of the things that were sold, and laid them at the apostles' feet, and they distributed to each as had need. (Acts 4:34-35)

Here is the Biblical pattern: first revival, then financial prosperity. Contrary to what some teach, we do not need money to have revival. Money should follow revival. If God has control of the hearts of the people, then he has their money, too. Note the above verses. *The revival in the early Church didn't cause these Christians to run out and purchase possessions and goods or lands and houses, but it caused them to sell these things!* You see, there's more than one way to look at financial prosperity. There are many facets of truth and angles of thought concerning money. What about stewardship and sacrifice? What about doing without so others can be blessed? There is a higher call and a higher level of consecration which is determined not only by how much you give away, but by how much (little) you keep (Mk 12:41-44). Jesus chose not to call on the Father for twelve legions of angels to deliver Him from a sure death (Mat 26:53) and our redemption. He chose not to heap up riches for himself. He chose not to accumulate this world's wealth. But He emptied Himself of everything for us.

And besides, as I mentioned earlier in this book, financial prosperity is neither a foundational doctrine nor a principle teaching in the Church. It is only a benefit just like healing, deliverance, protection, etc. Does that mean we shouldn't teach on finances or God's will for Christians to prosper? No, it just means we shouldn't place an extreme emphasis on it. Every believer should eventually walk in these blessings as a direct by-product of a consecrated and godly lifestyle. My fear is that we have majored on the minors and caused the hearts of many to go astray.

Poverty is not holiness. Gain is not godliness. But one thing is for sure: Greed will lead to grief.

Beware of hype, gimmicks, and manipulative tactics when it comes to money. Beware of so-called miracle offerings which don't go for

106

miracles at all. Beware of investing in Ishmaels that are not born of God, but of men. Invest in Isaacs. Ishmaels are birthed by negligent priests who fail to wait on God for the Isaac. Then those same Ishmaels are paid for by the offerings of naive and misinformed people who have been conditioned to give emotionally by the hyped up efforts of pitiful priests.

MOTIVES AND MEN

Because of the miracles he did in Jerusalem at the Passover celebration, many people were convinced that he was indeed the Messiah. But Jesus didn't trust them, for he knew mankind to the core. No one needed to tell him how changeable human nature is! (John 2:23-25 LB)

Many are the men who believe in God's *acts*, but who remain fickle because they don't know His *ways*. Many are they who are familiar with God's *house*, but so unfamiliar with God's *heart*. The Apostle Paul echoed the cause of the frequent mistrust he and the Lord Jesus had for men: *"For all seek their own, not the things which are of Christ Jesus"* (Phil 2:21). Yes, the love of God believes the best of people, but at the same time, it is not naive. In his humanity, every man is weak, frail, and his heart often deceptive. Even the greatest of God's servants have feet of clay. Even in man's great moments, Christ must remain the focus. "I am more afraid of my own heart than of the Pope and all Cardinals," Martin Luther said. (Hill, 1996. p. 21)

Multitudes followed Jesus. They heard his preaching gladly. They witnessed His mighty miracles. But they were fickle. One day they wanted to crown Him King and the next day they wanted to crucify Him. Jesus was constantly sifting the crowds. In the end when Jesus set His face like flint toward the cross and began speaking to them of the covenant (John 6:53-66) and of the identification they were to have with Him, the multitudes left along with some of His disciples. Even Peter, one of Jesus' closest disciples, rebuked Him for choosing the way of the cross. Jesus recognized the real source of this rebuke.

Get behind me, Satan! You are in my way, an offense and a hindrance and a snare to Me; for you are minding what partakes not of the nature and quality of God, but of men. (Mat 16:23 Amp.)

Beware of men who have no marks of the cross in their lives and preaching. They are diabolically aligned with the spirits of this age. They are "enemies of the cross whose god is their belly, and whose glory is their shame---*who set their mind on earthly things* (Phil 3:18-19)." They are self- deceived. There is a great truth to be told here. The closer Jesus got to the cross, the less people stayed with Him. The disciples tried to guard Jesus' life, but Jesus was guarding His death. If anything originated from man, Jesus wanted no part of it. "*I receive not glory from men - I crave no human honor, I look for no mortal fame*" (John 5:41 Amp). Compare the nature and quality of Jesus versus the religious leaders of His day: "*For they loved the praise of men more than the praise of God*" (John 12:43). In life and ministry, what are you hoping to receive? What are you craving? What are you really looking for? What is it that you wish from men? Is it their smile? Or do you long for self-denial? Jesus was dead to human praise, human criticism, and human opinion.

Listen to the frequent conversations at Christian conventions. It's all about men. It's all about who this one is and who that one is, who did what, and who's been where. Doesn't it get nauseating at times? Have you ever looked with holy eyes at some of today's most popular Christian magazines? It's all about conferences and camp meetings, special people and special programs, and how much we are all doing for the Lord. I realize some of these things have their *place*, but in all of it, where is His *face*? Don't you want to see Jesus? Doesn't it disturb you when some mere mortal stands in the way? Hide us, oh God in the cross of Christ!

The real truth about most men is this: They don't really know themselves as well as they think. We are never as submissive to God as we think we are. Listen, even Paul near the end of his earthly life and ministry had to be broken so that he wouldn't be puffed up with pride because of his many visions and revelations (2 Cor 12:7-9). Who do you think you are? Your only safeguard against pride is to walk in love toward God and toward man. Love never seeks its own. *True* men are men of selfless love. Paul said of Timothy, "*I have no one like him*" (Phil 2:20) because he was not self-serving or self-seeking. Paul also commended another *true* man:

"*...Honor men like him because he almost died for the work of Christ, risking his life to make up for the help you could not give me*" (Phil 2:29-30 NIV). Epaphroditus almost died through overwork to make up for the lack of service that the church gave to Paul. But here is the amazing thing about all this: Epaphroditus didn't want the church to know! He was distressed because the church heard that he was sick. Perhaps they would have felt bad for not being able to provide the service he rendered. What pure love and servanthood was in this man! He was seeking not his own glory, but the glory of the One who sent Him.

WHOSE GLORY ARE YOU REALLY SEEKING?

The origin of every word and action determines its glory and purity. Holy roots mean holy fruits. A desire for gain outside of God's will or even timing means you are worshipping a form of increase and success instead of God. It is evidence again that you are seeking your own glory and honor, and not the glory and honor of God. I call it unsanctified gain, which manifests in discontentment. Notice what true gain is:

Now godliness with contentment is great gain. For we brought nothing into this world, and it is certain we can carry nothing out. And having food and clothing, with these we shall be content. (1 Tim 6:6-8)

In the above context Paul is warning Timothy of men who imagine godliness to be a source of monetary profit and a means of making business. He is referring to men who enter ministry with wrong motives (v 5). Let me ask you a question. How many do you really know in ministry who are content with having food and clothing? It seems that there is so much striving for bigger and better positions, bigger and better possessions, bigger and better places, more and more power, influence, money, recognition, honor, success, etc. Will this merry-go-round ever stop? And when will its riders get off?

Is it wrong to have bigger and better or more and more? If it's outside of the will and timing of God, yes. It's idolatry and lust. I've heard well known ministers preach that God's will for us is just as much to be rich as it is to be saved. From whence comes such a persuasion? Paul spoke strongly against the desire to be rich (1 Tim 6:9). Riches are certainly not evil, but the desire to be rich is. What if the desire to be rich is for the sake of the gospel and for establishing God's kingdom on the earth? Well then, you would be rich toward God. But doesn't God give us all things richly to enjoy (1 Tim 6:17)? Friend, you're missing the whole point. Are the riches a result of gift or greed? Are you pursuing gain or godliness?

True godliness finds contentment in what it has today, and yet it knows that God gives increase tomorrow. But discontentment stopped Israel from obtaining the increase of their tomorrow. Their motives were wrong. They cried for meat when God gave them manna. True contentment comes from doing the will of God. That's the true meat which Israel refused to eat. Godliness with contentment would have brought Israel into the promised land, where abundance in every way would have been theirs to richly enjoy. But they were not willing to be tested that they might know what the true riches were. There is a difference between God truly blessing or giving you riches, and you getting them by your own self efforts. Be mindful that covetousness can also bring monetary gain, but it is ungodly gain.

Paul had learned the great secret of Christian maturity:

Not that I speak in regard to need, for I have learned in

whatever state I am, to be content: I know how to be abased, and I know how to abound. Everywhere and in all things I have learned both to be full and to be hungry, both to abound and to suffer need. (Phil 4:11-12)

When you're not content with what you have (not just in possessions, but in position, power, popularity, honor, recognition, influence, acceptance, approval, etc.) you'll be covetous in both your conduct and conversation. Then, what you say and do will be from a self-servitude and a seeking of your own glory (John 7:18). In both your words and actions you will be seeking gain for yourself.

A state of restlessness or discontentment is a breeding ground for deception. It's a place of never enough. It's a place of constant murmuring and complaining. In this state you frustrate God's grace and slowly grieve away His presence. True contentment is able to recognize that God is a God of increase and He will bring you forward, but only in His will, His way, and His time. The truly content person is also able to give thanks and rejoice for where they are and what they have *today*. God was bringing the children of Israel forward with plans of eventually taking them into the promised land, but they didn't like how He was doing it. They complained of the day to day provision of manna that God was giving them. They wanted more than He was giving them. They possessed an intense craving or desire for that which was outside of God's present will and timing (Num 11:4-6). They coveted and complained. They were filled with discontentment.

The one who seeks his own glory is covetous. Covetousness is a cancer which kills contentment. Conversely, contentment is the cure which kills covetousness. Covetousness fuels discontentment with yourself and weakens your spiritual life. Contentment fuels communion with God and strengthens your spiritual life. Discontentment fuels fleshly works and activity while contentment frees you from fleshly works and activity. Godly contentment is found in hearts who truly seek the glory and honor of God in everything they say and do.

The motive of the heart reveals the rightness or the wrongness of every thought, word, and deed. Are your thoughts true or are they false? Are your words true or are they false? Are your deeds true or are they false?

Whose glory and honor are you really seeking?

Chapter Twelve
FALSE HUMILITY AND CARNAL SUSPICION

Such regulations indeed have an appearance of wisdom, with their self-imposed worship, their <u>false</u> <u>humility</u> and their harsh treatment of the body, but they lack any value in restraining sensual indulgence. (Col 2:23 NIV)

The Word of God warns Christians against a false humility through legalism, angel-worship, and asceticism being taught by false teachers. There are many things we say and do which may appear to be done in humility but are, in fact, another form of pride.

There was a certain minister to whom God had committed a healing ministry to. It involved telling the people what God had said about this man's anointing in the area of healing. Basically, God's instructions to him were similar to what Jesus did in Luke 4:18. This minister was to declare to the people as Jesus did, that the Spirit of the Lord was upon him to minister healing. Well, being a bit conservative in his personality, this minister felt that this approach would draw too much attention to himself and seem like a prideful way to minister. In his desire not to appear proud, a false humility was at work. And false humility is pride. True humility is simply obeying what God has said to do. In the case of this minister, the real problem was his own image. He didn't want to appear proud. He was insecure. He was concerned about what people would think and say. The fear of man was actually birthing a subtler form of pride. Here again is the real root revealing our true heart -- the fear of man.

To walk in your God-given authority, you must get victory over the fear of man. Often the Lord will tell you to do something that goes totally against your own self-nature and personality so you can gain degrees of greater liberty and authority in your life. One time I saw a guest minister in a church run up to the pulpit after being introduced. I must admit, my first reaction to this strange act was one of disdain. Then the man asked the question that the entire congregation wanted to know: "Why did I run?" His surprise answer disarmed many, including me. "I don't know," he said. Then, pointing up, he added, "Ask Him." You see, he was responding spontaneously to what he believed was a simple directive from the Lord. Well, I'm not going to doubt the man's heart in the matter. Actually, after he explained himself to the people, I respected him for what he did, regardless of how strange it may have appeared. Although at first, this simple act appeared cocky and arrogant, it was really an act of true obedience, and thus humility. This man *valued* his obedience to the Lord over the desire to appear dignified before men.

Whatever one does that is truly as unto the Lord is acceptable to Him, whether or not it is popular and accepted by men. We cannot judge another person's heart. When David came to the front lines of the battle exuding confidence and faith in the living God (1 Sam 17:26), his older brother Eliab accused him of being irresponsible and proud.

Why did you come here? And with whom have you left those few sheep in the wilderness? I know your pride and the insolence of your heart, for you have come down to see the battle. (1 Sam 17:28)

Eliab judged David's heart, when in fact, it was Eliab who was jealous and proud. Perhaps he was still envious of David because Samuel had overlooked the tall, handsome firstborn of Jesse and anointed David in his stead (1 Sam 16:6-7). Eliab was suspicious of David because of the pride in his own heart. He thought he saw a *speck* in David's eye, but didn't realize he had a *plank* in his own (Lk 6:41). Eliab was a hypocrite whose eye was bad. A hypocrite is always suspicious of everyone else but himself. Because of his judgmental attitude, a hypocrite cannot see clearly (Lk 6:42). David's confidence in God was mistaken for pride and arrogance. Sometimes believers can be carnally suspicious of others because they, themselves don't walk in the same liberty, authority, and godly confidence others do. Carnal suspicion is often the result of a spirit of envy and jealousy in a person.

> *Then David said, "I will show kindness to Hanun the son of Nahash, as his father showed kindness to me." So David sent by the hand of his servants to comfort him concerning his father. And David's servants came into the land of the people of Ammon. And the princes of the people of Ammon said to Hanun their lord, "Do you think that David really honors your father because he sent comforters to you? Has David not rather sent his servants to you to search the city, to spy it out, and to overthrow it? (2 Sam 10:2-3)*

Again, here are some men questioning David's motives, but their supposed discernment was really carnal suspicion. These men were the princes of the people, rulers of the Ammonites, who were allies with the Moabites. The likely reason for their suspicion of David was that they were still angry over his harsh treatment of the Moabites (2 Sam 8:2).

Both Jesus (John 7:17-18) and the Apostle Paul (2 Cor 5:12) often had to explain their motives to their accusers, who were bound by superficial judgment. It was not spiritual discernment their accusers displayed, but carnal suspicion.

Do not judge according to appearance, but judge with righteous judgment. (John 7:24)

We cannot judge another person's life by external standards. Unless you know them after the Spirit, you cannot possibly begin to assume any judgment about their life. Author Rick Joyner shares this point so clearly concerning a minister he wrongly judged. I will share this example now as he did in his book.

> While attending a prophetic conference recently, I was with a brother I have known for years would be a

significant prophet to the last day church. This brother has been rejected by much of the church because of the status of his marriage, which has been one of many difficulties and at this time was in separation. One night the Lord spoke to me about my own marriage, which I consider to be in compliance with Biblical standards. He said that this other man was more righteous in complying with His mandate for marriage than I was. He proceeded to show me how I had been given a godly wife who loved and sought Him and that the condition of my marriage was purely the result of grace. I had given little effort to comply with His mandate in this and had been hard, unyielding and resistant to things He would have me do to improve my marriage. Against the most difficult humiliating circumstances and resistance, this other man had for years devoted himself to complying with the Biblical mandate and making his marriage work, even when he had every right, both Biblically and morally, to walk away from it. Yet, the church judged him as a failure and me as acceptable in this area. God has a very different opinion. (Joyner, 1989. p. 91-92)

Continually questioning other people's hearts and motives will eventually lead to a very critical spirit that will short-circuit God's presence in your life and even open a door to you being tormented by the devil. Even continually questioning your own pure motives will birth a strange kind of bondage to a false identity. Now we must always examine our hearts and make sure our words and actions are done in the sight of God, but this can be overdone by some Christians who are always finding reasons to doubt themselves and their own hearts. If you do this, condemnation will control your life. Allow the Holy Spirit to search your heart and bring things to your remembrance.

Jesse Penn-Lewis, a woman of prayer, planted seeds of doubt in the young Evan Roberts, used instrumentally by God to spark and lead the Welsh revival. When she succeeded in getting Evan to question his own motives, guilt and condemnation began to control his life. It led to a setback. Being self-conscious has a *sifting* effect on your nature. Conversely, being God-conscious has a *lifting* effect on you. *Self-consciousness is a subtle form of pride, insecurity, and inner weakness.* It is sin, and a reminder of what happened in the garden when Adam and Eve fell. They lost their sense of God-consciousness and became self-conscious. Fear, guilt, and doubt began to dominate their lives. This is what happens to us when we continually question our own motives and become too introspective. Eventually this breeds condemnation.

The balance we are attempting to present in this chapter is to neither be carnally suspicious of others nor walk in a false humility or pride. Don't read into another person's life because you don't know everything that is going on with him. Don't assume to know or even to understand because you are not in his shoes. One time I judged a young woman for being "stuck up" and snobby. She seemed so hard-hearted and unfriendly, and yet the very opposite was true. She was actually very gentle, joyful, and tender. The reason her outward appearance seemed hard was because she had lost her parents at an early age and was bounced from foster home to foster home. She had suffered much rejection and abuse, thus thwarting the development of her God-given personality. I asked the Lord to forgive me for misjudging and being carnally suspicious of her.

Remember, the devil is the accuser of the brethren (Rev 12:10). He is skilled at dividing Christians by speaking lies and vain imaginations to their minds concerning one another. It's sort of like what little children do to each other in school. One child will come up from behind another and hit him on the back and run. Meanwhile, the one child who was hit thinks it's someone else who was standing close by that hit him. This is what happens among people all the time, and Christians certainly aren't exempt from it. Someone will say one thing, but you'll think he meant something else. Or someone will do something or make a gesture, and you think he meant some evil by it, when in fact, he meant no such evil at all. And worse yet, the next time you see that person you are thinking about the evil that you thought he meant which you misinterpreted. Gradually, if you don't communicate with that person you build up a wall between yourself and them. From the other person's perspective, to further complicate matters, he may see you acting sort of strange every time you get around him so he draws back and begins to develop thoughts about you that may not be totally accurate either.

Misunderstandings and lack of communication are two tools the devil uses to cause division among believers. Lies, misunderstandings, and vain imaginations are all a result of carnal suspicions that people develop of one another because they do not walk in the love of God.

Let's look at how the love-ruled person responds to others in these types of situations.

Love is ever ready to believe the best of every person... (I Cor 13:7 Amp)

Love takes no account of the evil done to it---pays no attention to a suffered wrong. (1 Cor 13:5 Amp)

First of all, when it looks like, seems like, or even sounds like someone is doing you wrong, the love of God is prone to believe the best of the person involved. Secondly, if it is true, and not just a result of your carnal suspicion, then the love of God will still take no account of the evil or wrong done, or even pay attention to it. On the other hand, the scriptures do admonish that if a brother sins against you, then you are to go to him alone and tell him about it (Mat 18:15). And notice the reason for it---*to gain your brother.* God wants reconciliation and restoration. It doesn't even matter who is right or wrong. Notice it is not the erring brother or the one who has gone astray who goes to reconcile, but the one who has been sinned against.

Moreover if your brother sins against you, go tell him his fault between you and him alone. If he hears you, you have gained your brother. (Mat 18:15)

We must endeavor to walk in love and to *communicate* with one another, especially weaker brethren who are not as mature or skilled in discerning the devil's tactics and in using the Word of God. When the motive is love, far more reconciliation and restoration will occur in our relationships. I personally believe that we fool others, and sometimes deceive our own hearts, by false humility (which again is a subtle form of pride). And we also judge others prematurely and inaccurately because of carnal suspicions and wrong perceptions. These two things hinder us from being truly honest and transparent with each other, and greatly cut short the flow of God's love in our relationships with each other and in our churches.

And how will the world ever know we are Jesus' disciples if we have not this love toward one another?

Chapter Thirteen
OLD LEAVEN, NEW LUMP

Therefore purge out the old leaven, that you may be a new lump... (1 Cor 5:7)

Moreover if a brother sins against you, go and tell him his fault between you and him alone. If he hears you, you have gained your brother. But if he will not hear, take with you one or two more, that "by the mouth of two or three witnesses every word may be established." And if he refuses to hear them, tell it to the church. But if he refuses even to hear the church, let him be to you like a heathen and a tax collector. (Mat 18:15-17)

God is love (1 John 4:8), and love seeks to cover and conceal, not uncover and reveal anyone's sin. This means that the practice of all individual unrepentant sin should be first confronted privately before it ever becomes public. God's purpose is never to dishonor, embarrass, or humiliate an individual. Obviously, there are times and situations where sin must be exposed and confronted (outside of preaching on it), but only at the right *time*, in the right *way*, and with the right *spirit*.

Actually, before any believer confronts a brother who has sinned (and by the way, this is not just speaking of general sin, but either the practice of sin or a sin *against* you) he should first go to God in prayer on behalf of the person who has sinned. *"If anyone sees his brother sinning a sin which does not lead to death, he will ask, and He will give him life"* (1 John 5:16a). In prayer God will not only forgive him because you've asked, but you will develop a love for the sinning brother. Often God will also give us wisdom and revelation regarding the person's life or sin that will give us insight into how we should respond to him.

At times, especially when it concerns minor sins or character flaws in a person, one does not need to go to them. Often God will use such flaws in others to develop our own character and love. If it is something major that is jeopardizing the person's relationship with God, or it is a sin or offense against you, or it has the potential of causing problems in the church with other believers (especially the immature or new converts), then, after going to prayer about it, you should go to the sinning brother (or sister), in private. The purpose is to gain that brother and restore him.

Brethren, if a man is overtaken in any trespass, you who are <u>*spiritual*</u> <u>*restore*</u> *such a one in a spirit of gentleness, considering yourself lest you also be tempted.* (Gal 6:1)

Brethren, if anyone among you wanders from the truth, and someone <u>*turns*</u> <u>*him*</u> <u>*back*</u>*, let him know that he who turns a sinner from the error of his way will save a soul from death and cover a multitude of sins.* (Jam 5:19-20)

If your purpose is not to restore him, then you are not *spiritual;* therefore, you don't qualify as the person to restore him. That's what this scripture says. Restoration means a deliverance from sin and death. When you restore a believer living in sin or one who has been overtaken in a trespass, it's like winning someone to Jesus. It is most precious to the Lord. Don't take it lightly. But notice how you are to restore them---in a spirit of *gentleness,* so that you won't be tempted and also sin. You sin when you confront another's sin with a wrong motive or attitude. The purpose is not to prove him wrong and establish your own righteousness, or to even air out your differences, or release your own 'pent-up' steam, hurts, and offenses. Consider yourself. You are also one given to faults and sin. Beware that in attempting to remove a speck from your brother's eye you fail to see or to first remove the plank in your own eye. We need to ask God to cleanse us from all sin before we even approach another about their sin. That's another reason why we need to first go to God in prayer.

After going to God in prayer, you should then approach your sinning brother and not another person -- not even one in authority. As a matter of fact, when this principle is violated by going to the pastor or to another person in authority first, the response from them in authority should be, "Have you spoken to the other person first?" Bypassing proper relational steps violates a person's integrity, often over facts that were misunderstood and could have been cleared up by direct communication between the two parties. This way, teamwork and unity are not violated.

Now if the sinning brother refuses to turn and repent, then the next step would be to take one or two witnesses with you. God is so patient with us. If this next step also fails to bring repentance and deliver the sinning brother, then God calls for public confrontation (Mat 18:17).

> *And their message will spread like cancer. Hymenaeus and Philetus are of this sort, who have strayed concerning the truth, saying that the resurrection is already past; and they overthrow the faith of some.* (2 Tim 2:17-18)

> *Now I urge you, brethren, note those who cause divisions and offenses, contrary to the doctrine which you learned, and avoid them. For those who are such do not serve our Lord Jesus Christ, but their own belly, and by smooth words and flattering speech deceive the hearts of the simple.* (Rom 16:17-18)

> *But whoever causes one of these little ones who believe in Me to sin, it would be better for him if a millstone were hung around his neck, and he were drowned in the depth of the sea.* (Mat 18:6)

As you can see, it's a pretty serious thing when the practice of any form of sin (whether its immorality or doctrinal heresy or whatever) leads young believers into deception and destroys their faith. These verses serve as examples of how a person's persistent practice of sin can cause others to sin, their hearts to be deceived, and their faith to be overthrown. When someone's unconfessed and unrepentant sin and rebellion have this kind of effect on others, it is a serious spiritual crime of the highest degree. That's why Paul dealt so severely with sin in certain situations.

I wrote to you in my epistle not to keep company with sexually immoral people. (1 Cor 5:9)

Now this admonition probably came after other confrontations with this offender. It seems to me that the church, although having knowledge of this practice of sin, had not confronted this issue like Paul had instructed, or else why would Paul rebuke them for not doing so (1 Cor 5:1-2). Before arriving at this very serious level of discipline (v 3-5), Paul had instructed the church to disfellowship from this person (v 9), but apparently they didn't do it. The purpose of disfellowshipping with any sinning believer is so they will be ashamed, realize the seriousness of their sin, and repent. At this stage if the sinner still persists in his sin, and if it is causing others to also stumble and sin, to be deceived, or to overthrow their faith, then under proper apostolic and governing church authority, this more severe discipline could then be applied supernaturally.

There are more scriptures that give us this sort of instruction concerning our relationship to believers who practice sin.

But we command you, brethren, in the name of our Lord Jesus Christ, that you <u>withdraw</u> from every brother who walks disorderly and not according to the tradition which he received from us. And if anyone does not obey our word in this epistle, note that person and <u>do not keep company</u> with him, <u>that he may be ashamed</u>. Yet do not count him as an enemy, but admonish him as a brother. (2 Thes 3:6, 14-15)
Now I urge you, brethren, note those who cause divisions and

offenses, contrary to the doctrine which you learned, and _avoid_ *them.* (Rom 16:17)

Reject *a divisive man after the first and second admonition knowing that such a person is warped and sinning, being self-condemned.* (Tit 3:10)

We are instructed to withdraw, not keep company, avoid, or reject all sinning believers in the local fellowship. That is, after they've been confronted and warned. Like the church at Corinth, much of the church today has shown an indifference toward the practice of sin in their midst, and by sheer passivity has allowed the festering leaven of sin to further corrupt the work of God. Incest was being practiced among the church at Corinth, and they weren't doing anything about it! They were casual and conceding toward a practice of sin which could have ended in the damnation of a soul and the corruption of the church if the apostle Paul hadn't intervened.

You see, God instructed Israel during the Passover to remove all leaven from their houses. This practice is still observed today among Jewish people. Leaven's fermenting nature is symbolic of sin and evil's corrupting influence. The leaven of sin, evil, and hypocrisy can easily spread if left unchecked and undisciplined. And still, the proper order and relational steps must be maintained when the discipline is applied, or it won't be effective and produce the forthcoming fruit God desires.

For example, I'm thinking of a church right now whose pastors did fairly well to handle a difficult situation involving the practice of sin in the church, but because of the lack of thoroughness in the overall discipline process, they lost many families in the church. The sin was adultery involving a young woman and a married man who was separated from his wife. Both this young woman and this legally married man claimed to be Christians and a part of this fellowship. When confronted privately about their sin, both of them refused to change. They were finally asked to leave the church. I believe, however, that these pastors erred when they failed to confront this sin publicly in front of the church.

Eventually, this couple returned with the woman, now pregnant, and still cohabiting with this married man. She went around the church and told everybody how God had blessed her with this baby, all the time showing no shame or remorse for her sin. Meanwhile, the man was calling the pastor and threatening to bust up the church, accusing the pastors of being unloving and hypocritical. To complicate matters, the young pregnant lady's mother, who was also a part of this fellowship, was bringing her to church despite the pastor's wishes. And because of their twisting of the real truth of this entire situation, many other minds in the church were poisoned with their lies. The final outcome of this was that it caused much division in the church and heartache to its pastors; many families left the church, and the pastor's authority suffered further undermining.

Our loyalty must not be to people, but to the truth. Some families in this church, including the mother of the young adulterous woman, sided with her even though she was continuing the practice of an immoral lifestyle. They did not stand for the truth, but made a peace treaty with blatant sin and rebellion. It doesn't matter if the person in sin is an immediate family member or a relative. Right is right and wrong is wrong. Some believers do not possess this kind of integrity. They can't be trusted, especially in a position of authority. Why? Because they will always show prejudice and partiality toward people instead of being loyal to the truth.

Even the elders were not exempt from being publicly rebuked.

> *Do not receive an accusation against an elder except from two or three witnesses. Those who are sinning rebuke in the presence of all, that the rest also may fear. I charge you before God and the Lord Jesus Christ and the elect angels that you observe all these things <u>without prejudice, doing nothing without partiality</u>.* (1 Tim 5:20-21)

Heaven stands behind the Word of God. Heaven opposes sin. Heaven backs church discipline administered by proper governing church authority, done in an attitude of love according to the scriptures, and under the Lordship of Jesus Christ.

Why is this subject so vital? Because when we allow sin to fester, it corrupts the unity of the church. It was when the early church was found in one accord that great things happened (Acts 2:1, 4:24, 5:12). Unity is a result of love, obedience, and true holiness. Those who persist in sin and have hidden agendas taint the spiritual atmosphere of a church body. It's a leaven that corrupts.

Unity is a product of the atmosphere created by the purity of hearts. Believers in the early church were of one heart and one soul (Acts 4:32). They even sold their houses and lands and used the monies to support each other and the church (Acts 2:44, 4:32, 34-35). In comparison to the unity and the glory they experienced, how pale and dim is ours! The holy qualities of these early disciples leave us much to be desired in the modern church. The strength of their glory and unity was the reason the sin of Ananias and Sapphira was judged so severely. There was too much at stake. The apostles and the early church had a responsibility to protect the glory. If that particular sin had been allowed to fester, it would have been as leaven, which if left unchecked and undisciplined would have greatly weakened the glory and power in the early church.

No church is perfect, sinless, or flawless. No person or group of people is completely free of sin and imperfections. I also know that there will always be young converts in our midst that may be carnal and still a little worldly, but God looks on the heart and only requires them to walk in what they know. If the motive of the heart is right then they will add to the unity and power of the church and not take away from it.

Oh yes, as time went on the early church had its problems with sin and strife, but it was constantly being confronted. False doctrine and heresies threatened their purity too, but you can't deny these godly characteristics that contributed to their power and glory. As I've said elsewhere in this book, God is not expecting absolute perfection, and He only judges us according to the knowledge that we have. You are only required to walk in what you know. You are only accountable for the limited revelation that you have. The early church constantly had an influx of new believers coming in, and yet for awhile, anyway, they remained so powerful. Oh, for the restoration of such a people and such a church! Oh, for the glory that they knew and experienced, and more!

Here is what the church of today needs to sorely understand, and with the right spirit, make consequent adjustments. The fellowship of the early church was not all inclusive. There was a standard of fellowship that was maintained by the apostles throughout the early church era. Professing Christians had to maintain that standard to remain in the fellowship. Immoral persons were not permitted to stay (1 Cor 5:9); neither were those who were unruly and walked disorderly (2 Thes 3:6). The other believers in the church were commanded to withdraw from them and not keep company with them. Those who defiled their separation from the world (Jam 4:4) were to be excommunicated by divine command. Domineering and sectarian leaders were also excluded (3 John 9-11). Fellowship was also based on the acceptance of the doctrine of Christ (2 John 9-11). Why are we so lax on these things when the Word is not?

The apostles exercised divine discipline, thus removing wicked persons from their midst so that the purity and unity of the church would not be corrupted. This brought great fear and reverence for God within the church and prevented an infiltration of evil into it (Acts 5:11-14).

Therefore let us keep the feast, not with old leaven, nor with the leaven of malice and wickedness, but with the unleavened bread of <u>sincerity</u> and <u>truth</u>. (1 Cor 5:8)

In the chapter "Motives and Values," I gave a definition of the word "sincerity" from the NKJ version of the Bible from the above scripture. Let me give a part of it to you again. Think of holiness and unity when you hear this definition. Think of purity of heart. Think of corporate atmosphere and corporate power. Are you ready? Here it is: One of the meanings is "a transparent honesty, genuine purity, manifested clarity, and unsullied innocence." Repeat that first definition real slowly, and think about the meaning. Now get excited about this next part. This word "sincerity" describes *one who does not fear thorough examination of his <u>motives</u> <u>and</u> <u>intents</u>, because he has <u>nothing</u> <u>to</u> <u>hide</u>.* Glory to God!

Friends, this definition is the picture of the unleavened bread of which the church is to be. This is the new lump. Based on the motives and intents of our hearts we can get to a place where we are not afraid of being examined because we have nothing to hide! This is the divine and holy order that is to be in our hearts. When this quality of corporate heart is found in our midst, I believe that's when we will see the glory and power of God like we see it in the book of Acts, and more, for the glory of the latter house shall be greater! Can you imagine it? I can!

Nothing to hide, nothing to hide, nothing to hide! If they put the real motives and intents of your heart up on a big screen on Sunday morning in a church service, would you want to hide? I wonder - is a big screen what the apostle Peter saw when Ananias and Sapphira stood before him in their sin? Is a big screen what Nathan the prophet saw when David killed Uriah to cover his adultery with Bathsheba? Is a big screen what Elisha saw when his servant Gehazi took a bribe? Well, I've got news for you. God has a big screen. We are not dealing with a Peter, or a Paul, or a Nathan, or an Elisha! We are dealing with Almighty God!

And there is no creature hidden from His sight, but all things are naked and open to the eyes of Him to whom we must give account. (Heb 4:13) We better have nothing to hide now, or one day, like our sinful parents Adam and Eve, we'll be ashamed of our nakedness (Gen 3:10-11). The Word, the Blood, and the Spirit agree. Our only hope is purity of heart. This is the glory that covers. This is the *new lump*.

Being honest and naked before Him now will cover you with His glory. Covering up your sin now will later find you naked (Pr 28:13).

Get naked now, and you'll never be ashamed.

Chapter Fourteen
THE DAY OF DISTINCTION

Many are called, but few are chosen (Mat 16:20). *Many* got offended by the teachings and demands of Jesus and left (John 6:66). In the last days *many* shall be offended and deceived, and the love of *many* shall wax cold (Mat 24:10-12). *Many* who heard the teachings of Jesus and ate and drank in His presence were not saved (Lk 13:23-26). *Many* sought to enter through the narrow gate but were not able. *Many* who call Jesus Lord and even do wonderful works in His Name will not enter into the kingdom of heaven (Mat 7:21-23). And *many* who are first shall be last (Mk 10:31).

Many false prophets shall arise (Mat 24:11); false brethren (2 Cor 11:26), false apostles (2 Cor 11:13), and false teachers, too (2 Pet 2:1). One day the false will be separated from the true. The weeds will be separated from the wheat (Mat 13:38-43). The bad fish will be separated from the good fish (Mat 13:47-50). The goats will be separated from the sheep (Mat 25:31-46). And the foolish virgins will be distinguished from the wise virgins (Mat 25:1-13). Will you be in or will you be out? Will you be grateful or will you be full of grief?

As the Day of Judgment and distinction approaches, some will say, "All things continue as they were" (2 Pet 3:3-4). Nothing has changed. "Where is the promise of His coming (v 4)?" Some will continue to eat, drink, buy, and sell (Lk 17:28). They'll act totally indifferent to the urgency of the hour. They will live like Jesus is not coming. They will continue on in their daily routine and act like they will never be judged. These are all symptoms of a form of godliness that repeatedly denies the power to change (2 Tim 3:5). But the scriptures warn us that the Master will come in a day when some are not looking for Him and in an hour that they are not aware (Lk 12:48). The scriptures also say that when Jesus appears, some will be ashamed because they will not be found abiding in Him (1 John

2:28). But everyone who has the hope of His revelation purifies himself (1 John 3:2-3). Will you be pure or will you be defiled? Will you be received or will you be denied?

Some have religion but not righteousness. Some have doctrine but they are not doers. Some only have a form but no fire. Some even talk about heaven but they're closer to hell. The difference between them and the world no one can tell. I read a survey of recent statistics from this past decade revealing that 30% of all professing Christians don't read the Bible, 35% don't pray, 75% don't give or get involved with missions, and 95% have never led anyone to Christ.

There are basically three types of "Christians": *Nominal,* or in "name" only; *residual,* or those who live on yesterday's manna and move of God; and the *on fire,* totally in love with Jesus, Spirit-filled ones. The latter are the ones God knows. They love Jesus more than anyone and anything. These are the ones who will walk with Jesus in white, for they are worthy (Rev 3:4). Jesus said that anyone who is not loyal to Him above all else is not worthy of Him (Mat 10:37-38). And anyone that has left their first love has fallen and needs to repent (Rev 2:4-5).

We must cultivate and guard our love for Jesus diligently. We must keep our affections turned toward Him. It's easy to let that slip, especially in the busy-ness of life and ministry. The following story illustrates this well.

Satan called a worldwide convention. In his opening address to his evil angels, he said, "We can't keep some Christians from going to church. We can't keep them from reading their Bibles and knowing the truth. We can't keep them from conservative values. But we can do something else. We can keep them from forming an intimate, abiding experience in Christ. If they gain that connection with Jesus, our power over them is broken.

"So let them go to church. Let them have their conservative lifestyles, but steal their time so they can't gain that experience in Christ. This is what I want to do, angels. Distract them from gaining hold of their Savior and maintaining that vital connection throughout their day!

"How shall we do this?" shouted his angels.

"Keep them busy in the non-essentials of life and invent unnumbered schemes to occupy their minds," he answered.

"Tempt them to spend, spend, spend, then, borrow, borrow, borrow. Convince the wives to go to work and the husbands to work 6 or 7 days a week, 10-12 hours a day, so they can afford their lifestyles. Keep them from spending time with their children. As their family fragments, soon their homes will offer no escape from the pressures of work.

"Over stimulate their minds so they cannot hear that still small voice. Entice them to play the radio or CD player whenever they drive, to keep the television, the VCR, and their CD's going constantly in their homes. And see to it that every store and restaurant in the world plays music constantly. This will jam their minds and break that union with Christ.

"Fill their coffee tables with magazines and newspapers. Pound their minds with the news 24 hours a day. Invade their driving moments with billboards. Flood their mailboxes with junk mail, sweepstakes, mail order catalogues, and every kind of newsletter and promotional offering, free products, services, and false hopes.

"Even in their recreation, let them be excessive. Have them return from their recreation exhausted, disquieted, and unprepared for the coming week. Don't let them go out in nature. Send them to amusement parks, sporting events, concerts, and movies instead. And when they meet for spiritual fellowship, involve them in gossip and small talk so that they leave with troubled consciences and unsettled emotions.

"Let them be involved in soul-winning. But crowd their lives with so many good causes that they have no time to seek power from Christ. Soon they will be working in their own strength, sacrificing their health and family unity for the good of the cause."

It was quite a convention in the end. And the evil angels went eagerly to their assignments, causing Christians everywhere to get busy, busy, busy, and rush here and there.

Has the devil been successful? You be the judge.

All of us, no matter what our service to the Lord may be, must continually watch over our hearts' affections for Jesus. I read recently about a very well known minister. He has been all over the world and has personally prayed with over two million people to receive Jesus. His ministry is marked by great signs and wonders. He has seen the dead raised, the lame walk, the deaf hear, and the blind see. Early in his life with the Lord, he had such a sweet relationship with Him that God's abiding presence was upon him day and night for eleven years.

But recently, in tears, he said that in the last few years he had gotten so busy with ministry that he had left that first love he once had for Jesus. Somewhere along the way, he had lost that passion for Him. He was still fervent about winning souls. He was still committed to the call of God on his life; yet he had been drawn away from Jesus Himself.

He hadn't realized it until a few months ago when he went to conduct some meetings in another country. There he found the Christians aglow with that abiding presence of God. Their faces shone with joy and love for the Lord. When they worshiped the Lord, this minister just wept and wept because he recognized in these people the very thing he once had but lost.

You say, "How can this happen to us?" I don't have all the answers, but I know one thing---the heart is a very vulnerable place. It needs to be guarded constantly. And the older you grow and the higher you go in your call, the more this is so. Keeping your heart is the biggest job you'll ever have in life (Pr 4:23).

I know two things about everyone's life and future. If Jesus tarries, both of them will surely come to pass. One day you will die. And one day you will stand before God. You will only be known by your supreme love for Jesus.

Nothing else will matter then. Nothing else should matter now.

Chapter Fifteen
HOLY FEAR, HOLY FIRE

Now therefore, <u>fear</u> the Lord, serve Him in sincerity and in truth... (Jos 24:14)

For everyone will be seasoned with <u>fire</u>, and every sacrifice will be seasoned with salt. Salt is good, but if the salt loses its flavor, how will you season it? Have salt in yourselves, and have peace with one another. (Mk 9:49-50)

The fire of holiness burns in your heart in proportion to the fear of God you possess. After all, the fear of the Lord is to depart from evil (Pro 16:6). And the one who *departs* from evil is the one who *delights* in holiness.

There were five foolish virgins and five wise virgins. Foolishness is sin. Wisdom is holiness. A wise man fears and departs from evil (Pr 14:16). That's why a wise man's lamp keeps on burning while a fool's lamp eventually goes out (Mat 25:8).

We all know that fire purifies. Well, so does the fear of the Lord. It's in the fear of the Lord that you are cleansed from all filthiness of the flesh and of spirit. It is in the fear of the Lord that your heart is purified and holiness is perfected in your life (2 Cor 7:1). The fear of the Lord causes every component of your character to stand God's inspection and meet His approval. It will establish your heart blameless in holiness (1 Thes 3:13).

Jesus said if your hand or foot causes you to sin, cut it off. If it is your eye that causes you to sin, pluck it out (Mk 9:43-48). It is better to enter into life maimed than having two hands, two feet, and two eyes, and go to hell. What did Jesus mean? He is not talking about self-mutilation, but self-discipline and self-denial. It is better to deny yourself now and experience pleasant pain than to spend eternity in hell's flames. While verses 43-48 speak of hell fire, I believe that the seasoning with fire spoken of in Mk 9:49 will either be hell fire or holy fire depending on the person's response. Notice it says, *"Everyone* will be seasoned," or "salted," or "tested" as some translations say. The fire of God will either purge you or devour you depending on your response.

The Scripture tells you to present your body a living sacrifice, holy and *acceptable* unto God (Rom 12:1), but it is only by His grace and holy fear that you can serve God *acceptably*, for He, our God, is a consuming fire (Heb 12:28-29). *God consumes sacrifices of holy fear.* When there was order in the old temple, the fire came down (2 Chron 7:1). Divine order in the new temple, the heart of man, will produce the same results. *Hearts full of grace and holy fear are hearts full of holy fire.*

It was when Elijah repaired the altar (1 Kings 18:30) and obeyed the word of the Lord (v 36) with right motives (v 37), that the fire fell (v 38). Elijah obeyed because he feared the Lord. Therefore the Lord sent the fire.

It was a Friday night and the evangelist was preaching another one of his fiery messages on the sins that so easily beset us, especially in the summertime that was fast approaching. He made mention of sexual lust which burns in many men during the summer season. He encouraged men to stay away from naked and promiscuous scenes that would ignite their lustful passions. The very next day my family and I had already planned to go to the beach.

We drove and drove until we found an uninhabited spot on the sandy shores. Even so, once in awhile a woman in a bikini would come walking our way. I would turn my neck or close my eyes long enough until she passed. I never looked. I never lusted. I was in pursuit of holiness through the fear of God. Because this was my heart's motive, God gave me grace to victory. I had plucked my eye out. This is what

Jesus meant.

Truth and sincerity of heart attracts grace. There is grace to *will* and grace to *do*. The moment you say, "I *will* obey God. I *will* deny myself. I *will* confess and forsake my sin," then there is grace to act. Do not frustrate the grace of God by excessive self-efforts. God's holy fire and salt will season you (purge) only when your heart turns toward Jesus and away from fleshly lusts. But, you say, "My spirit is willing, but my flesh is weak." Then humble yourself and receive more grace. If you really hate your sin or your habit, then be encouraged, the fear of God is already at work to perfect holiness in your life (Pr 8:13).

Lack of surrender hinders grace. Lack of surrender is evidence that you still own your own life. *"You are the salt of the earth; but if the salt loses its flavor, how shall it be seasoned? It is then good for nothing but to be thrown out and trampled underfoot by men"* (Mat 5:13). A Christ-like spirit of self-denial is what flavors the earth. Otherwise, you who were meant to be the salt of the earth become good for nothing.

I know your works, that you are neither cold nor hot. I could wish you were cold or hot. So then, because you are lukewarm, and neither cold nor hot, I will vomit you out of my mouth. (Rev 3:15-16)

The church of Laodicea was lukewarm, and neither hot nor cold. This has often been interpreted as if *hot* meant *godly enthusiasm* and *cold* meant *ungodly antagonism,* but there is another explanation which suits the historical and geographical context better. Laodicea was situated between two other important cities, Colossae and Hieropolis. Colossae, wedged into a narrow valley in the shadow of towering mountains, was watered by icy streams which tumbled down from the heights. In contrast, Hieropolis was famous for its hot mineral springs which flowed out of the city and across a high plain until it cascaded down a cliff which faced Laodicea. By the time the water reached the valley floor, it was lukewarm, putrid, and nauseating. At Colossae, therefore, one could be refreshed with clear, cold, invigorating drinking water; at Hieropolis, one could be healed by bathing in its hot, mineral-laden pools. But at Laodicea, the waters were neither *hot* (for health) nor *cold* (for drinking).

In other words, the basic accusation against the church of Laodicea is that it was ineffectual, and good for nothing. The Laodicean church brings neither a cure for illness nor a drink to soothe dry lips and parched throats. The sort of Christianity represented by the Laodicean church is worthless. The church did not provide refreshment for the dry and thirsty nor healing for the sick and was consequently distasteful to the Lord. Thus, the church is not being called to task for its spiritual temperature but for the barrenness of its works. This explains Christ's statement: *I wish that you were cold or hot.* He is not saying that outright apostasy is preferable to middle-of-the-roadism, rather He is wishing that the Laodicean Christians have an influence upon their society.

Salt losing its savor means selfish motives without God's favor. Selfish ambition was a big problem among the disciples. In their desire to be the first and the greatest (Mk 9:33-35) their salt was losing its flavor. Strife was spoiling the seasoning and making the salt good for nothing. *"Have salt in yourselves, and have peace with one another."* (Mk 9:50)

Let's talk about salt. Vine's Expository Dictionary says this:

> Being possessed of purifying, perpetuating and antiseptic qualities, salt became emblematic of fidelity and friendship among eastern nations. To eat of a person's salt and so to share his hospitality is still regarded thus among the Arabs. So in scripture, it is an emblem of the covenant between God and His people, Num 18:19; 2 Chron 13:5; so again when the Lord says "Have salt in yourselves, and be at peace with one another" (Mk 9:50). In the Lord's teaching it is also symbolic of that spiritual health and

140

vigor essential to Christian virtue and counteractive of the corruption that is in the world. It was to be offered with all offerings presented by Israelites, as emblematic of the holiness of Christ, and as betokening the reconciliation provided for man by God on the ground of the death of Christ. (Lev. 2:13) (Vine & Bruce, 1981. p. 315)

Based on the above, here are some enlightening qualities about salt.

1. It purifies and perpetuates.
2. It speaks of fidelity (loyalty) and friendship.
3. It is an emblem of the covenant between God and His people.
4. It is symbolic of spiritual health and vigor essential to Christian virtue.
5. It is counteractive of the corruption that is in the world.
6. It is emblematic of the holiness of Christ.

Amazingly, these are all qualities that the fear of the Lord helps to work into our lives. *I believe the fear of the Lord to be a key ingredient that seasons you with holy fire and salt.*

Over and over in the Mosaic books there is written the expression, "a sacrifice made by fire, of a sweet savor unto the Lord" (Ex 29:18, Lev 8:28, Num 29:6,13,36). Jesus gave Himself for us as an offering and a sacrifice to God for a sweet smelling savor or fragrance (Eph 5:2). Paul spoke of the fragrance of Christ that was manifested through him and others (2 Cor 2:14-16). Do you see a pattern here? The sweet smelling savor and fragrance is released by the giving of ourselves as an offering and a living sacrifice. I believe when we offer ourselves in love for the glory of God there is a divine flame released in our hearts that lights up incense which ministers to the Lord. This is the acceptable sacrifice *made by fire.*

Scripture also speaks of heaven having golden bowls of incense, which are the prayers of the saints (Rev 3:8). Acceptable prayers come from consecrated lives. God hears prayers bathed in holy fear. In the garden of Gethsemane in His most trying hour, Jesus cried out to God and *was heard because of His holy fear* (Heb 5:7-9). With "fear and trembling" is how we are to walk worthy and work out our salvation (Phil 2:12). The man who trembles at God's Word and obeys His voice is the one whose words mean something to the Lord.

I came to send fire on the earth, and how I wish it were already kindled! But I have a baptism to be baptized with, and how distressed I am till it be accomplished! (Lk 12:49-50)

The fear of God caused Jesus to endure a great baptism of suffering. But the fire of God fell to the earth as a result. The fear of God caused Jesus to obey and the fire to stay.

Both Elijah the prophet and his successor Elisha spoke this phrase: *"As the Lord God of Israel lives, before whom I stand..."* (1 Kings 17:1; 18:5; 2 Kings 3:14; 5:16). Paul the Apostle penned this similar statement: *"For we are not, as so many, peddling the word of God; but as of sincerity, but as from God, we speak in the sight of God in Christ"* (2 Cor 2:17).

In both Elijah's and Paul's day, as it is today, many false prophets and false apostles peddled the Word of God. However, Elijah and Paul ministered in "the sight of God." They were men of sincerity and truth, who feared God and hated covetousness. Such were the qualifications for leaders as far back as the time of Moses.

Moreover you shall select from all the people able men, such as fear God, men of truth, hating covetousness; and place such over them to be rulers of thousands, rulers of hundreds, rulers of fifties, and rulers of tens. (Ex 18:21)

The pattern is *clear.* It must begin with leaders *everywhere.* Draw near to God and you affect the *atmosphere.* The fruit of pure and clean hearts is pure and clean *air*.

The fire of God that purifies is *holy fire*. The fear of the Lord that cleans is *holy fear* (Ps 19:9).

Chapter Sixteen
HOLY BONDAGE, HOLY LIBERTY

It has been said that liberty to your spirit is a bondage to your flesh, while liberty to your flesh is a bondage to your spirit. This is true, but let us uncover a deeper truth. *There is a holy bondage.*

And see, now I go <u>bound</u> <u>in</u> <u>the</u> <u>spirit</u> to Jerusalem, not knowing the things that will happen to me there, except that the Holy Spirit testifies in every city, saying that chains and tribulations await me. But none of these things move me; nor do I count my life dear to myself... (Acts 20:22-24)

Early in my Christian walk I had a love for the Lord, but I did not fully understand what it really meant to fear Him. Because of the famine for the word of the Lord on true holiness, and because of the errant "grace" theology that I was taught, I failed the Lord many times. The Word of God that I was hearing was not working in me a real strong hatred for sin. Thus, I grew lax and loose toward certain sins and habits.

In the early 1980's when I was first saved, a certain group of preachers were loud on righteousness, emphasizing positional truths and "in Christ realities" which were a tremendous blessing to my life and walk with God. There was an overabundance of teaching on what I call the *legal* side of redemption. But hardly ever did I hear preaching on sanctification and holiness and being separated from the world, or what some would call the *vital* or experiential side of redemption. As I grew spiritually I began to discern that there was a diabolical silence on the subject of true holiness. Preachers talked about putting on the fruit of the new man without ever mentioning putting off the deeds of the old man. The cure for sin was proclaimed, but the cause and the consequences were hardly ever named. And so I developed a hunger for holiness.

There were two extremes I found in the church that still are very much a problem today. One extreme was that the subject of grace was understood to *forgive* our sins, but not to *free* us from them. According to this philosophy, our old man still controlled us and we were only sinners saved by grace. There was no victory. There was no freedom. Whenever holiness was preached, it was usually without an understanding of grace or faith and it led to legalism. We were convinced of our sin, but never of the righteousness we had in Christ. Therefore, Christians remained under condemnation and defeated so in order to compensate for their need of righteousness; they developed an external standard of righteousness based on works and rules. This is called *legalism*.

The second extreme I found, which we have already briefly mentioned, was in the overemphasis of an imbalanced grace and faith teaching without the important ingredients of repentance and holiness. Under this teaching we are righteous in Christ and are never to be sin-conscious. Sin is a thing of the past. We are now overcomers under grace. It became taboo in some places to even mention the word sin. Often soft substitutes like 'mistake' or 'problem' were used in place of sin. In some circles it actually became a sin to confess sin or any weakness or lack. Simply put, without the anchor of repentance and an understanding of true holiness, the teaching of faith and grace were twisted and misunderstood, and it led to presumption, sin, and compromise among many believers. This second extreme I call *licentiousness*.

Deception entered in more than some people even realize today. There is no doubt in my mind concerning the following statement which to me identifies the root of deception in certain segments of the body of Christ in the last two or three decades. Here it is: *Faith to save your life has been preached, thus positioning grace to be used as a license to sin.* It has led to lightness and looseness in the lives of many believers.

Legalism and *license* are at two opposite sides of the pendulum.

Liberty is what's supposed to be in the middle. But even in that, many have become *loose,* misusing their liberty (Gal 5:13), and letting it become a stumbling block to the weak (1 Cor 8:9). We are admonished to walk in the light as He is in the light (1 Jn 1:7). *True light and true liberty never lead you into legalism, licentiousness, or looseness.* It's true that some will judge your liberty (1 Cor 10:29), but it is equally as true that some will be judged for their abuse of liberty. Our liberty must be aligned with God's holiness and used to perform His will, and not our own. Paul said that he was at liberty to eat meat sacrificed to idols, but wouldn't do it as long as the world stands if it caused a weaker brother to be offended (1 Cor 8:13). How can any Christian hurt or offend anyone in the name of liberty? Holy liberty is ruled by love. Or to put it another way, *love steers liberty.* We are bound to the king of laws which is love (Jam 2:8). *Holy liberty means holy bondage.*

Consider Paul. If there was anyone who understood true love and true liberty, it was him. He understood that where the Spirit of the Lord is there is liberty (2 Cor 3:17). He told the Galatians to stand fast in their liberty (Gal 5:1), knowing full well that there were some who were spying out their liberty (Gal 2:4). Yet in that same letter to the Galatians, he warned them not to misuse their liberty (Gal 5:13). Paul understood liberty. He understood what it meant to be free. But Paul also referred to himself as a slave or a bondservant (Tit 1:1; Rom 1:1; Phil 1:1). In other places he called himself a prisoner of Christ Jesus (Philemon 1:1; Eph 3:1, 4:1). And he wasn't just referring to being in a physical jail. Paul was a spiritual prisoner bound to the will of God for his life, whatever that meant. He was a prisoner of Christ, and bound by the Holy Ghost. Notice how our opening text reads in the Amplified translation:

> *And now, you see, I am going to Jerusalem, <u>bound</u> by the (Holy) Spirit, and obligated and compelled by the [convictions of my own] spirit, not knowing what will befall me there; except that the Holy Spirit clearly and emphatically*

affirms to me in city after city that imprisonment and suffering await me. But none of these things move me; neither do I esteem my life dear to myself, if only I may finish my course with joy, and the ministry which I have obtained [entrusted to me by] the Lord Jesus...(Acts 20:22-24 AMP)

Neither imprisonment nor suffering, not even death could stop Paul from finishing his course and fulfilling the ministry he received from the Lord. You see, Paul did not consider his life his own. He, like any literal slave, belonged to His Master. He had no rights to do anything or go anywhere without his Master's consent. *The Lord was his owner.* Paul had been delivered from a *demonic* bondage into a *divine* bondage. His earthly life was not *dear* because heaven was so *near.* He lived near the *cross* because he'd counted all things *loss.* The reason Paul was so *brave* was because he was a *slave.* Oh, for such slaves in this *hour* to do God's will and carry forth His *power!*

Now consider Peter. He knew something about liberty and bondage. After all, it was Peter who wrote about the slaves of corruption who promised liberty, while with the same stroke of pen also writing that a man is in bondage to whatever has mastered him (2 Pet 2:19). And again in one breath Peter writes and warns not to use liberty as a cloak for evil, but as *bondservants* of God (1 Pet 2:16). Although Peter was one of the original apostles of the Lamb, and the leader of the early church, he also counted himself as a bondservant of Jesus Christ (2 Pet 1:1).

Finally, consider James, the Lord's brother. He apparently did not believe in Jesus during His entire ministry. Jesus even appeared to him after His resurrection (1 Cor 15:7). Now remember, James grew up in the same home with Jesus. Long before Jesus was ever anointed for public service James knew him. They grew up together and played together as children. They were brothers with the same earthly parents. Consider this also. Years after the resurrection of Jesus, it appears that James became the pastor or key leader in the church at

Jerusalem (Acts 15). In actuality, he was an apostle. And yet in his letter inspired by the Holy Spirit he chose not to refer to himself as anything but a bondservant or a slave of Jesus Christ (Jam 1:1). Interesting, isn't it, how James was also another one who spoke about the law of liberty (Jam 2:12)?

A liberty that does not produce a holy bondage is a false liberty. How can you say that you're more than a conqueror (Rom 8:37) when you won't even deny yourself? How can you declare that Christ is your righteousness (1 Cor 1:30) when you don't even walk in righteousness? How can you say you love God when you don't even love your neighbor? Who can boast of dying for Jesus when they're not even living for Him? The grace of God is greatly hindered for lack of the fear of God. The fear of God will lead to obedience.

There are certain often-repeated phrases in the church world today that create soft attitudes in believers if not tempered with a fuller truth. One is this: "God loves you the way you are." That is a true statement, but it often produces not only liberty, but license as well. Of course God loves you the way you are unconditionally, but He loves you too much to leave you the way you are. God's will is for each of us to be more and more transformed into the image of His Son Jesus Christ.

Here's another one: "God loves you and has a wonderful plan for your life." That is absolutely true. But again, we must ask ourselves, what is a wonderful plan? Is it the American dream of wealth and happiness? Is it the safe and secure life within the comforts of our luxurious homes? The apostle Paul was told early on from the time of his conversion that he would suffer greatly for the cause of Christ (Acts 9:15-16). Peter was told that he would die a martyr's death (John 21:18). Jesus promised persecution to His other followers as well (Mat 10:17-22). Was this God's wonderful plan for their lives?

Today when some believers don't get the provision or blessing they want from God they are so quick to doubt His love for them. With all the trials and opposition they had, I often wonder how in the world these early martyrs even knew that God loved them. For them, the cross of Jesus Christ was enough. God had already proven His love there. The cross was a symbol of liberty for them, but also a symbol of the debt they owed. Holy liberty again meant holy bondage.

The above statements are true, but they often create a liberty with license instead of a holy bondage to God's complete will.

Joseph was sold into Egypt as a slave thousands of years ago. Today there are still some hidden places where slaves are bought and sold, and used for cheap hard labor or now, sex. But a holy slave cannot be bought or sold. He belongs to the Supreme Master. A holy slave is not hired but is a willing volunteer. He does not do cheap labor, but it is the costly kind that he embraces--the kind that sometimes costs much blood and many tears, the kind that comes with great service and noble sacrifice.

Holy slaves are the only ones who are truly free. Nothing in this world binds them. No man owns them. Holy slaves are wholly bound to one certain sound. They live each day to *hear* their Master say, "You are my son (or daughter) in whom I am well pleased." They live with eternity in full view. They're running in a *race*. They're picking up the *pace*. They're pressing for the *prize*. They know the end is near when they will look into His *eyes*. This hope keeps them *pure* (1 John 3:2-3), and so their entrance is *sure*.

Are you a holy slave?

Chapter Seventeen
KEEPING THE MOTIVES
OF YOUR HEART PURE

Keep your heart with all diligence, for out of it spring the issues of life. (Pr 4:23)

The greatest job we will ever have as Christians is to keep our hearts right before God. The deepest part of our hearts is our motives. No one can see your motives, or the reason you think, say, or do certain things. Only God can see the real reason behind our thoughts, words, and actions.

Most people at one time or another will twist words or events to their own advantage, covering over the real truth to put themselves in the best light, often using people for their own gain or to protect themselves. Nearly everyone has ulterior motives or something they keep secret and hidden from others.

The only relationship that is completely pure and free from false hidden motives or agendas is that of the heavenly Father and His Son, the Lord Jesus Christ. The fellowship they share is all in the light, and there is no darkness in it at all. They have a totally transparent relationship. And that transparency is the nature of true holiness. This is the kind of holiness that is worthy of our pursuit.

Purity of heart is purity of love. The Lord loves each of us like that. The Lord has never taken advantage of anyone or used them for personal gain. The Lord is completely transparent toward us in thought, word, motive, and deed, and we are to be like Him and be that way toward one another.

Of course it is much easier to be transparent toward the Lord because you know that He won't hurt you. But in order to be pure and transparent toward one another we must become vulnerable and even be willing to suffer hurt and misunderstanding at times just as our Master did.

I believe that all the judgments of God are based on our motives and purity of heart. God's judgments are based on the real reason behind everything we think, say, and do. It is very sobering to think of our lives in that way, isn't it? This is why 1 Corinthians 13 tells us that everything not done in love, even the most sacrificial acts, will profit us nothing.

So how then can we keep our motives pure and cultivate purity of heart, purity of love, and transparency in our lives?

The very first step is to make Jesus your first love (Rev 2:4-5). Intimacy with the Lord is the pathway toward purity of heart. Longing for a closer walk with the Lord will keep your heart turned toward Him. This position has a purifying effect on your life.

When you love Jesus with all your heart it is easier to love your neighbor as yourself with the purest of motives. Furthermore, it is much easier to keep your eyes on Jesus when he is truly your first love. Many people have their eyes on man, and that is the reason the devil is always sifting them. When your eyes are on man you will constantly compare yourself to others and measure yourself against them and what they are doing. This causes a *sifting* in your life instead of a *lifting*. This is how Christians fall from their God-given authority. Then their motives become tainted. The remaining steps that follow are all rooted in keeping Jesus as your first love.

Secondly, always be a servant. One day my son asked me how to be more likeable to his peers at school and church. I told him to take more of an interest in their lives and let the love of God flow out to them. In other words, it is as you forget about yourself and concentrate on being a servant to others and take an interest in others that your love becomes pure. Jesus taught his disciples that the servant of all is the greatest of all. This is true authority.

Thirdly, mind your own business. Once again, when you meddle in the affairs of others and you start measuring yourself in the light of others, you will start losing your God-focus and your peace. This will affect your heart's motives because you have taken your eyes off the Lord. Rejoice in your own labor and in the will of God for your own life even though it may be very different from that of others. Focus on your own personal growth in the Lord and your assignment and what He has told you to do.

When your eyes are on other people you will either feel inferior or superior to them. This will give birth to either envy or pride. You will either feel like a failure or a success. Both of these positions are wrong. When I was younger in the Lord I saw in a vision a large green snake wrapped around me. It represented a certain envy I had toward the outward success of others especially those who were called to the ministry like I am. The Lord told me that if I would wrap myself around Him that snake could not wrap itself around me.

Early in my Christian life and ministry I got in the habit of constantly comparing what I was doing and how I was living against that of others. This caused a state of unrest in me and it frustrated the grace of God. The Lord showed me how to overcome that and those instructions are highlighted here in this chapter.

Be careful you don't measure yourself against others but against the Word of God and the light you've been given. Jesus Christ is your standard and not man.

Finally, realize that God's reward system is based on faithfulness and not on competition through performance. Basing God's love on your performance will keep you striving and measuring your efforts against those of others. Pride and selfish ambition will rule your life as you seek to compete and outdo others.

Obedience is what God requires. He will reward your obedience, and not necessarily your performance or your sacrifice.

When you do these things you will find peace and fulfillment growing in your spirit as your motives become purified.

Notice again these two verses that are listed in the beginning of this book.

For we must all appear and be revealed as we are before the judgment seat of Christ, so that each one may receive [his pay] according to what he has done in the body, whether good or evil, [considering what his purpose and motive have been, and what he has achieved, been busy with and given himself and his attention to accomplishing]. (2 Cor 5:10 AMP)

Now if anyone builds on this foundation with gold, silver, precious stones, wood, hay, straw, each one's work will become clear; for the Day will declare it, because it will be revealed by fire; and the fire will test each one's work, of what sort it is. If anyone's work which he has built on it endures, he will receive a reward. If anyone's work is burned, he will suffer loss; but he himself will be saved, yet so as through fire. (1 Cor 3:12-15 NKJ)

2 Corinthians 5:10 in the Amplified Bible speaks of the purpose and motive of the heart as being a key ingredient at the judgment seat of Christ. 1 Corinthians 3:12 speaks of six kinds of building material. Three are found hidden under the earth (gold, silver, and precious stones) and three are above the earth (wood, hay, and stubble). The motives of our hearts are hidden and no one can see them.

Gold is symbolic of your total life in Jesus Christ. Gold represents your heart, your personal faith in Christ, and your devotion to Him. *"I counsel you to buy from Me gold refined in the fire, that you may be rich..."* (Rev 3:18). Scripture compares a pure heart to pure gold which has been refined. A pure heart is tender and soft just like pure gold is in its most refined form.

Silver represents your words. *"The tongue of the righteous is as choice silver..."* (Pr 10:20). Jesus said that out of the abundance of the heart the mouth will speak, and man will be judged for every idle word that comes out of his mouth (Mat 12:34-37). This is the reason that our words are so important. They are measuring sticks for what is in our hearts. Therefore it makes perfect sense that our words would be a standard for being judged.

Precious stones were put on the breastplate of the Old Testament priests so they could carry the people close to their hearts (Ex 28:17-21) This is symbolic of one's prayer life.

Notice that gold, silver, and precious stones are all in some way connected to the heart. And once again, our motives are the deepest part of our hearts and represent the basis for all judgment - so keep your heart pure for out of it spring the issues of life (Pr 4:23).

Conclusion
LOVE: THE MIGHTY MOTIVATOR

The motivational *revelation* that always brings a behavioral *revolution* in our walk with God is the love of God. When a person knows he is loved and valued, chances are he will never quit. Children who receive constant love and affirmation at home are much more likely to succeed once they're out on their own. The gospel of Jesus Christ places the highest value on humanity than any philosophy this world has ever known.

I remember hearing the story of a young prostitute whose father was her pimp. Can you imagine? When she was gloriously saved her father went into a fit of rage. Even though this young woman was born again, she had no sense of value or worth. She felt like a commodity and had a difficult time believing that Jesus had forgiven her. She felt unloved, dirty, and rotten. All day long she'd bathe herself constantly to try to feel clean. One night she couldn't sleep because the voice of the Spirit overwhelmed her. All night long she heard the words ringing in her heart, "You are accepted in the Beloved, you are accepted in the Beloved, you are accepted in the Beloved!" The Holy Spirit had persuaded her of her righteousness before God. The voice of love, acceptance, and affirmation set her free and *motivated* her heart to serve Jesus.

The demands of the gospel are great, but the grace, love, and mercy displayed toward us by God are even greater. It is the goodness of God that leads a man to repentance (Rom 2:4). People change and respond to the demands of Christ when they feel they're worth something. Demanding obedience without demonstrating love and providing grace to obey can lead to hurt, bitterness, and anger. By grace we are saved (Eph 2:8) and it is by grace we continue to stand (1 Pet 5:12). God works *in* us as His love is revealed *to* us.

For it is God who <u>works</u> <u>in</u> <u>you</u> both to will and to do of His good pleasure. (Phil 2:13)

Now may the God of peace who brought up our Lord Jesus from the dead, that great Shepherd of the sheep, through the blood of the everlasting covenant, <u>make</u> <u>you</u> <u>complete</u> in every good work to do His will, <u>working</u> <u>in</u> <u>you</u> what is well pleasing in His sight, through Jesus Christ, to whom be glory forever and ever. Amen. (Heb 13:20-21)

A man's concept of God and His love and grace will determine the depth of his walk with God. Do you have a revelation of God's love for you? The only way a person can personally and intimately know of God's love for him is by the revelation of the Holy Spirit, and by an ever increasing experience.

I have a friend I will call Fred who shared this awesome encounter he had in the Lord. There was a time in Fred's life when he was very depressed and reached the point when he was going to take his own life. He sat in a chair in his living room holding a loaded revolver pointed to his head. With one last plea of desperation Fred called out to God, "God, if you are out there, please show me that you really care!" Suddenly the phone rang. Fred answered and heard the voice of a Christian friend who was out driving around and felt compelled to call Fred. This friend shared how he sensed such an urgency to let him know of God's love for him. Fred's heart broke and he began to cry. God had demonstrated His overwhelming goodness and mercy toward him. Needless to say, Fred did not commit suicide but instead gave his heart to God. The love and goodness of God led him to repent. When a sense of value and worth was realized by Fred, then his heart responded to God.

We love Him because He first loved us. (John 4:19)

There are many things that can harden the heart of a person and keep them from knowing and receiving God's love. Anger, un-forgiveness, bitterness, resentment, regrets, offenses, hurts, fears, and disappointments keep many from receiving the love of God.

God will usually minister acceptance and affirmation to such a person before ministering any kind of discipline. And then He will encourage and speak to his potential as He did to Peter.

And he brought him to Jesus. Now when Jesus looked at him, He said, 'You are Simon the son of Jonah. You shall be called Cephas' (which is translated, a stone). (John 1:42)

And the more that's given to a person, the more revelation they have of God's love, then the more is required of them and the more they can easily respond and return that love.

Most assuredly, I say to you, when you were younger, you girded yourself and walked where you wished; but when you are old, you will stretch out your hands, and another will gird you and carry you where you do not wish. (John 21:18)

Jesus first spoke to Peter's potential at the beginning of His earthly ministry. Then at the end Jesus prophesied by what kind of death Peter would glorify God (v 19).

God's great love was not only displayed on the cross long ago (John 3:16), but it still speaks to us afresh and anew today. Hear His voice today and harden not your heart (Heb 3:7-8). Let His love and goodness motivate and provoke you to purity of heart and purity of service.

REFERENCES

Blessitt, A. (1985). Arthur, a Pilgrim. Hollywood: Blessitt Publishing.

Bounds, E. M. (1972). Power Through Prayer. Grand Rapids: Baker Book House.

Brown, M. L. (1993). It's Time to Rock the Boat. Shippensburg: Destiny Image Publishers.

Finney, C. G. (1984). How to Experience Revival. Springdale: Whittaker House.

Finney, C. G. (1996). Power From on High. Springdale: Whittaker House.

Hill, S. (Ed.). (1993). On Earth as it is in Heaven: A Classic Bible Reading Guide. Shippensburg: Destiny Image Publishers.

Hill, S. (1996). Time to Weep: The Language of Tears. Foley: Together in the Harvest Publications.

Jowett, J. H. (1905). The Passion for Souls. New York: Fleming H. Revell Co.

Joyner, R. (1989). The Harvest. Pineville: Morningstar Publications.

Joyner, R. (1996). The Final Quest. New Kensington: Whittaker House.

Liardon, R. (1998). Smith Wigglesworth Speaks to Students of the Bible. Tulsa: Albury Publishing.

Lindsay, G. (Ed.) The New John G. Lake Sermons. Dallas: Christ for the Nations, Inc.

Tozer, A. W. (1969). Gems from Tozer. Harrisburg: Christian Publications, Inc.

Vine, W. E., & Bruce, F. F. (Eds.). (1981). Vine's Expository Dictionary of Old and New Testament Words. Grand Rapids: Fleming H. Revell.

ABOUT THE AUTHOR

Bert M. Farias, together with his wife Carolyn, graduates of Rhema Bible Training Center, founded Holy Fire Ministries in 1997 after serving for 9 years as missionaries in West Africa establishing nation-changing interdenominational Bible training centers with an organization called Living Word Missions.

From 1999-2003 Bert served as the internship coordinator on the senior leadership team of the Brownsville Revival School of Ministry and Fire School of Ministry in Pensacola, Florida, a school birthed from a massive heaven-sent revival that brought approximately four million visitors from around the world with an estimated 150,000 first time conversions. There Rev. Farias and his wife taught and mentored young men and women in the call of God and trained them for the work of the ministry.

Bert is a missionary evangelist carrying a spirit of revival to the Church and the nations. An anointing of fire marks His ministry with frequent demonstrations of the Spirit and the power of God. With a divine commission to also write, Bert has authored 6 books with an emphasis on helping to restore the true spirit of Christianity in the Church and its leaders and preparing the saints for the glory of God, the harvest, and the soon return of the Lord.

Before being separated to the full time preaching and teaching ministry, Bert experienced a unique and powerful baptism of fire. His consuming passion is for human beings to come into a real and vibrant relationship with the Lord Jesus Christ through the power of the Holy Spirit and to become passionate workers in His kingdom thus preparing them for the second coming of Christ, being among the wise virgins and a part of the first-fruits harvest who will be received into glory and receive a sure reward.

Bert currently resides in Windham, New Hampshire with his beautiful wife Carolyn and sweet son of promise Daniel.

OTHER BOOKS BY BERT M. FARIAS

SOULISH LEADERSHIP

This book is for everyone…

- Who longs for purity of heart.
- Who desires to be set aright in the core of his being.
- Who dreads God's disapproval more than man's.
- Whose greatest phobia is the fear of a wasted life and burned-up works.

The works that endure the testing of God's holy fire will one day be rewarded. Others will suffer loss (1 Cor 3:12-15). Will your works stand the fire or will they go up in smoke? In that day the motive of every heart will be made clear. Leaders will be judged by a higher standard. Only one question will matter then, and it's the same question that matters now: Are you building your kingdom or the kingdom of God?

THE JOURNAL OF A JOURNEY TO HIS HOLINESS

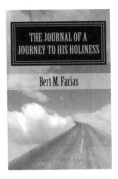

This journal-style book is not your normal run-of-the-mill literary work. Rather, it is a mystery from heaven unveiled---a saving word----a blueprint of the mind of God for every minister and saint. This journal will take you to a school beyond the veil wherein the Holy Spirit himself is the instructor.

The content of this journal reads like a tapestry woven byan unseen hand into the multi-colored fabric of each page. Its timeless truths and priceless principles will demand your prayerful attention; indeed a rare find for this day and age.

Don't just read this journal, but let it read you. Allow it to impregnate you with a depth of holy desire for intimacy and unbroken fellowship with the Father of spirits. There is a great purging and cleansing God wants to do in this hour in his Church, especially among ministers. This journal is one of those sign-posts that definitely point the way.

THE REAL SPIRIT OF REVIVAL

In this book, Bert challenges the status quo of Christianity today and redefines its true spirit which is one of revival and of living the Spirit filled life. With one eye on the coming glory of the Lord and His soon return, and anothereye on the harvest of souls yet to be reached, *The Real Spirit Of Revival* takes the reader into a preparation to becoming a true lover of Jesus and a passionate worker in His kingdom. These vital truths that dot each new chapter of this book are sure to awaken you as one from a deep sleep, and light a fire in your soul.

If you are tired of a mundane relationship with God and desire to burn with His holy fire this book is a must read.

THE REAL GOSPEL

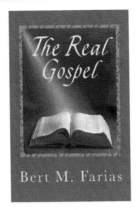

With piercing prophetic insight this book exposes the fallacies and shortcuts in the modern gospel and calls us back to Jesus and the cross. Its message reveals why so many Christians and churches today lack power, endurance, and character. Written in the spirit, style, and plainness of speech of the old timers, it breathes into today's shallow gospel the life of the spirit of holiness, giving us fresh eyes on old truths.

This is a critical book for the hour – a real wake up call to all. Backed by an abundance of scripture *The Real Gospel* is as truthful as it is radical.

THE REAL SALVATION

Can you imagine feeling secure in a salvation you don't even possess? Such is the state of mass humanity today. We have libraries full of sermons yet still so much confusion and deception about what the real salvation is. With poignancy and pinpoint clarity this short and sweet book cuts through the fat of satanic philosophy, exposes the deception of the broad way of religion, and shines the light on the narrow path to eternal life.

Most books are 200 pages with 30 pages worthwhile, and 170 of fluff. *The Real Salvation* is less than 60 pages, but every word counts. Make it count for you and your unsaved friends and loved ones!

TO ORDER ANY OF THESE BOOKS VISIT OUR WEBSITE

www.holy-fire.org

OR AMAZON BOOKS.

MINISTRY INFORMATION

To become a monthly partner with Holy Fire Ministries, schedule a speaking engagement with Bert, or to receive the ministry's free newsletter please contact:

Holy Fire Ministries
P. O. Box 4527
Windham, NH 03087

Web: www.holy-fire.org

Email: adm@holy-fire.org